A Walk with Nature is a marvelous a(
poetry. As it promises in the title, it do(
even more, links the reader with the n
resources do. After reading this splendi ......, ...,....... ....
on a nature walk in search of the peak experiences I felt while diving
into the nourishing poetry that is its gift to all of us. I recommend *A
Walk with Nature* wholeheartedly to all who wish to connect and
reconnect with the animating force of nature. It is truly a treasure.

Charles Garfield, PhD
Clinical Professor of Psychology for 40 years at UCSF Medical School
Author of *Life's Last Gift: Giving and Receiving Peace When A Loved
One Is Dying*

Psychotherapists listen and help people who come to them to talk of
their fears, hopes, dreams, and despair. I think of what we do as soul
work. "Psyche" is a Greek word for "soul" and poetry is soulful. Here
is a collection of poems chosen by psychologists who read and write
poetry themselves and know when the psyche is speaking. Like music,
only in words, a poem can express and in some way validate our own
inarticulate feelings of being and belonging in nature and the
universe.

Jean Shinoda Bolen, MD
Jungian analyst, activist, (jeanbolen.com)
Author of *Goddesses in Everywoman, Close to the Bone, The Millionth
Circle*

While facts and figures are important for our understanding the
natural world, poetry is the key that unlocks the gate and allows us to
step into the living landscape of frogs, trees, stones and creeks. If
language is our way of describing the world, poetry gives it life. I
applaud those who conceived and compiled this book of poetry. It is
another fresh breath offered to sustain this beautiful, breathing world.

Betsy Perluss, PhD
Wilderness Guide
School of Lost Borders

In reading this book you cannot help but encounter the objectivism of nature. Yes, it is beautiful. Yes, it should be explored. However, this misses the heart of what *A Walk with Nature* is about: an authentic relationship with nature. As an Arapahoe saying teaches, "All plants are our brothers and sisters. They talk to us and if we listen, we can hear them." This book guides you through encounters that offer a deeper connection with nature, one grounded in awe and reverie. At the end of this journey you may just know not only nature but yourself a bit better.

Trent Claypool, PsyD
Licensed Psychologist
Director of Sport and Mental Performance
Neurofeedback Colorado Springs

A Walk with Nature:
Poetic Encounters that Nourish the Soul

Michael Moats
Derrick Sebree, Jr.
Gina Subia Belton
Louis Hoffman
Editors

University
PROFESSORS PRESS

Colorado Springs, CO
www.universityprofessorspress.com

A Walk with Nature: Poetic Encounters that Nourish the Soul
Edited by Michael Moats, Derrick Sebree, Jr., Gina Subia Belton, and Louis Hoffman

First Published in 2019, University Professors Press. United States.

ISBN 13: 978-1-939686-48-0

University Professors Press
Colorado Springs, CO
www.universityprofessorspress.com

Front Photo "Kauri Tree" by Michael Moats
Cover Design by Laura Ross

Dedication

To my dad, Jesse, for taking me as a small child to the front porch with you and sitting with me through my fear of thunderstorms. To this day it is now one of my favorite activities and has become a source of grounding and relaxation.

~ Michael Moats

To the memory and spirit of my mother-in law and uncle. Your compassion, love, and kindness touch my heart every day. Your laughter and love stay with me to this day. Thank you both for such wonderful gifts.

~ Derrick Sebree, Jr.

To my dear friend and husband Marc. Your Bodhisattva heart shined so bright across the stream, that day you held out your hand and said, "Just jump, I've got you." Your Apollo spirit to my indigenous soul enlivening Artemis, we will always run and play together in the rivers and the forest with our Totem Salmon.

~ Gina Subia Belton

To the many dogs who have accepted me as their person and kept me grounded in nature and spirituality: Amaya, Dante, Aryia, and Kalee.

~ Louis Hoffman

Poetry, Healing, and Growth Series

Stay Awhile: Poetic Narratives on Multiculturalism and Diversity
Louis Hoffman & Nathaniel Granger, Jr. (Eds.)

Capturing Shadows: Poetic Encounters Along the Path of Grief and Loss
Louis Hoffman & Michael Moats (Eds.)

Journey of the Wounded Soul: Poetic Companions for Spiritual Struggles
Louis Hoffman & Steve Fehl (Eds.)

Our Last Walk: Using Poetry for Grieving and Remembering Our Pets
Louis Hoffman, Michael Moats, and Tom Greening (Eds.)

Poems For & About Elders (Revised & Expanded Edition)
Tom Greening

Connoisseurs of Suffering: Poetry for the Journey to Meaning
Jason Dias & Louis Hoffman (Eds.)

Silent Screams: Poetic Journeys Through Addiction & Recovery
Nathaniel Granger, Jr. & Louis Hoffman (Eds.)

Waterfalls of Therapy
Michael Elliott

About the Poetry, Healing, and Growth Series

Poetry is an ancient healing art used across cultures for thousands of years. In the Poetry, Healing, and Growth book series, the healing and growth-facilitating nature of poetry is explored in depth through books of poetry and scholarship, as well as through practical guides on how to use poetry in the service of healing and growth. Poetry written with an intention to transform suffering into an artistic encounter is often different in process and style from poetry written for art's sake. In this series, there is engagement with the poetic greats and literary approaches to poetry while also embracing the beauty of fresh, poetic starts and encouraging readers to embark upon their own journey with poetry. Whether you are an advanced poet, avid consumer, or novice to poetry, we are confident you will find something to inspire your thinking or your personal path toward healing and growth.

Series Editors,
Carol Barrett, PhD; Steve Fehl, PsyD; Nathaniel Granger, Jr, PsyD; Tom Greening, PhD; and Louis Hoffman, PhD

For Susan—
Thank you for walking
and leading a healing
journey for me (and others).
Thanks for helping me
to stay Awake!
With Love +
Gratitudes
Lynn

Table of Contents

Acknowledgments

We would collectively like to thank University Professors Press for partnering with us in allowing a community of voices and experiences to be shared with others through this anthology. We also would like to thank that community, the authors of the poems, that have honestly, creatively, and vulnerably offered their lives through poetry. Additionally, we want to share our appreciation for the contribution of artwork by Stephen Linsteadt and Richard Bargdill. An additional thank you goes to Justin Lincoln for his reflection on being in nature and the freedom of connecting relationally. His approach to utilizing the activities transcends the stated means of using them in a creative, personal way. He lives as he speaks.

Michael: I would like to thank my wife, Annie, for always being supportive in my dreams and desires, as well as understanding when I sometimes say I want to walk alone in nature and allow whatever experience I have to form as I meander along. I would also like to thank my parents for instilling creativity in my life and for living that example.

Derrick: I would like to thank those who have supported, loved, and struggled with me along my journey. First and foremost, my wife, Vanessa, your unending love, support, and guidance are precious treasures I hold close. We share a bond that is unyielding and eternal, one that gives me strength, courage, and fills my heart with joy. My soulbrother, Don; my mother, Stephanie; my father, Derrick Sr.; and loving relatives: you all have helped me become the person I am today. Your struggles and efforts to give me the best in life are labors of love which guide me, filling me with passion to impact the world.

Gina: I would like to give deep gratitude for the rivers and mountains, the orchards and grape fields of the mighty San Joaquin Valley of California—your indigenous heart continues to beat in my own along with our Ancestors, who still perfume the air above and enrich the soil below. Many thanks to Marc Daniel Belton, a friend for 35 years; we have walked a long road together and I couldn't have asked for a better companion on the journey. We have suffered well together, husband, and so we have loved better, in all of the wild places. Our children, precious daughter Miquette Angelina and her husband James Thompson, your tenderness and lightness of being is our home together, in the forest, mountains, the trees, the ocean and our totem Salmon. And last but most important, to my colleagues, friends, and collaborators, Michael, Derrick and Louis, I offer many warm bows for your patience with my struggles with chronos; it can be difficult to keep up when one is immersed in a life of kairos! You have been more than gracious with my steep learning curve with some of the technology but in the end, we arrived. Together. This opportunity to grow with you all in nature will always be a heart-full experience to me.

   Xotla cueponi!

Louis: I would like to thank the majestic Colorado mountains and wilderness that have repeatedly helped me connect with myself and with nature. I also would like to thank my many dogs over the years— Amaya, Dante, Aryia, and Kalee—who often bring me back to nature and remind me of so many of the wonders that I often miss in the routine of daily life. My family—Heatherlyn, Lakoda, Lukaya, and Lyon—you are my world and my appreciation goes to you every time I engage in another writing project. There are many friends who often are a part of my writing through their presence and encouragement in my life: Nathaniel Granger, Jr., Brittany Garrett-Bowser, Robert Murney, Jason Dias, Glen Moriarty, Shawn Rubin, Richard Bargdill, Theopia Jackson, Kirk Schneider, Ed Mendelowitz, Michael Moats, and many more. Last, I want to thank my fellow editors of this volume, Mike, Derrick, and Gina, for the collaboration and for patience as my schedule often did not allow for as much time as I would have liked.

Foreword

The editors of this volume of poetry provide a compelling introduction to the place of poetry and nature in growth and healing capacities. The diverse range of poems and poets speaks to both "Who heals the healer?" and how mental health professionals help their clients through painful transitions. Life is a series of losses (e.g., relocation, career changes, relationships, death, physical abilities, natural forces, and so much more) but also opportunities for personal and interpersonal development. Nature (plants, animals, landscape) offers ecological lessons on life and living. This collection is consistent with humanistic theory and practice in that it reaches the cognitive, affective, behavioral, and spiritual aspects of our human experience. This contributes to meaning making and a holistic view of life.

Poetry and a poetic approach to life offer us access to a special connection, especially during these troubled times: the presence of what is good, enduring, and inspiring in life.

Consider, for example, a few lines from the Desert Dweller (Cynthia Anderson):

> The desert has died and come back
> ten thousand times and will not
>
> let you forget—every last creature
> inhabits you, part of you.

The power of poetry and the written word drawing from nature is clearly evident in this collection. Hope is embedded in the poems by capturing and validating what we think and feel. Through the context of human nature and the human condition, the poems let us know that we are not alone. In effect, creativity contributes to health and healing through some of our natural surroundings. It is apparent that the editors recognize that poetry is one of the arts but is also research of the highest order. Note the lines from *Forms and Products* (Ndaba Sibanda):

the singularities of the physical world
the wonders of the plants and animals

....

old age or diseases or spells or natural causes?
we try to understand the nature of a problem

This collection of poems and exercises is well suited for the three major domains of poetry therapy: 1. Receptive/prescriptive: reading/listening and responding to poetry. 2. Expressive/creative: engaging the participant in expressive writing (e.g., poetry, journal, letters) 3. Symbolic/ceremonial: poetry and poetic activities to honor and/or affirm a life transition (Mazza, 2017). The poems read (receptive/prescriptive) can also be a catalyst for written expression (expressive/creative) and may prove to be symbolic/ceremonial (e.g., writing a letter to a deceased loved one, reciting a poem at a sacred natural setting).

This volume reactivated a sense of my own transitions. As a father and grandfather "Play with Me" resonated with my heart. My 4-year-old grandson (as did my daughter and son) often picks up leaves, branches (twigs), and small stones to examine. And I continue to learn about the importance of little things.

Consider some lines from "Play with Me" *(Roseanna Gaye Ross):*

Come--
Play with me--
We'll skip over rain puddles,
Sing nonsense songs,

....

But, the child has grown into the man, the woman...
Our fields and forests are lost from life's map.

...

And yet, a voice,
calling out softly
coaxes...
Come--
Play with me--

While enjoying my time with my adult daughter playing with my 4-year-old grandson (who often takes me by the hand to come play with him), I can still hear "Come play with me" from my son, who died in a car crash at the age of 21. Peace and hope come with a visit from a cardinal flying past us.

I also recall from 1978 in a poetry therapy session with an adolescent client who brought tiny seashells that she collected at the beach and put them in a small bottle for me. I didn't realize it at the time but she was engaged in self-healing through nature. That little bottle still has a place on my bookshelf.

As the editors note, the process of healing and growth is a lifelong journey. The unfinished aspects of poetry are particularly noteworthy. The reader completes the poem with each new reading over time. And the responses often change over time. Writing in response to some of the poems in this volume can provide a release of emotions and contribute to gaining control over anxiety and depression. This collection is an engagement with the beauty of poetry and nature; and a call to action—as simple and small as walking with a child through the woods and as global as dealing with climate change. Science is real, but sometimes it takes poetry and the arts to bring the message home.

References

Mazza, N. (2017). *Poetry therapy: Theory and practice* (2nd ed.). New York, NY: Routledge

Nicholas Mazza, Ph.D., is Professor and Dean Emeritus at Florida State University, College of Social Work, Tallahassee, FL. Dr. Mazza holds Florida licenses in psychology, clinical social work, and marriage and family therapy. He has been involved in the practice, research, and teaching of poetry therapy for over 40 years. Dr. Mazza is the author of *Poetry Therapy: Theory and Practice, 2nd Edition,* and editor of a four-volume series, *Expressive Therapies* (published by Routledge). He is also the founding (1987) and current editor of the *Journal of Poetry Therapy: The Interdisciplinary Journal of Practice, Theory, Research, and Education.* In 1997, Dr. Mazza received the *Pioneer Award* and, in 2017, the "Lifetime Achievement Award" from the National Association for Poetry Therapy.

Introduction:
Walk with Us

Nature is ever at work building and pulling down, creating and destroying, keeping everything whirling and flowing, allowing no rest but in rhythmical motion, chasing everything in endless song out of one beautiful form into another. (Muir, 2018, Chapter 3, ¶31)

The living Earth takes many forms and names, such as Terra, Mother Earth, and Gaia. Often, people describe Earth as nature or the environment. Various cultures around the world speak to the sacredness of humanity's relationship with the natural world.

Many of my (Michael) mornings begin by observing the transitional silence of the night transforming into the warm, dimly glowing horizon that starts upon the awakening cue of the songbirds. Fluttering of wings in a nearby bush, the rustling of leaves disrupted by the scurrying rodents dodging the potential flight paths of the birds of prey, and thermals bringing warmth to the once cold darkness. A new day holds remnants of yesterday but with no concern for the past. What a beautiful canvas, a template for living.

As beautiful as this sunrise is, it will exist for a short time before it transforms into day and back into the darkness of night, another reminder. Some will focus solely on the sunrise, some the day, and some the night. Some also will see this experience as an observer of a glorious show rather than a part of the greater existence in unison. However, nature offers an endless education into the interdependent relationship of all it entails. Nature not only sustains, nourishes, and exists within humanity; we also look to it for its healing wisdom. This healing process can take many forms—mirroring the many faces, phases, and cycles of the living planet. Nature holds life and death within it, cradling them both in a fierce embrace of awe.

To give voice and space to these moments of healing with nature, the editors of *A Walk with Nature* have assembled a diverse collection of poems. This anthology illuminates the lived engagement, education, and relationship of many varied yet interconnected voices that have dared to commune with nature beyond an observational enjoyment.

It is our hope that the reader goes beyond reading for entertainment or even simply feeling in order to allow a connection to what is being presented in a way that fosters growth, change, and further exploration of the self, of nature, and of one's interconnectedness to one's world (see *Listening to Bees*). Our interconnected and interdependent relationship with nature is not a new idea or philosophy; it has been a historical part of indigenous societies.

Balance, Relationality, Co-creation: We Have Always Been Eco-psychological—An Indigenous Perspective

Archetypal and Depth Psychologist, James Hillman (2017) wrote:

> To what does the soul turn that has no therapist to visit? It takes the troubles to the trees, to the riverbank, to an animal companion, on an aimless walk through the city streets, a long watch of the night sky. Just stare out the window or boil water for a cup of tea. We breathe, expand, and let go, and something comes in from elsewhere. (p. 88)

For millennia, the first therapists for many humans were, in fact, trees, rocks, riverbanks, and purposeful walks through landscapes both welcoming and treacherous. These territories were traversed by a confused, inspired, or heavy heart, carried by the instinct that contact with nature would bring healing, hope and/or inspiration *from elsewhere*. A walk with nature in these moments sought balance.

A balanced relationship with the phenomenal world that is often referred to as nature is embraced by many Indigenous societies, and with such rigor that a landmark mental health agenda was declared in 2016. Working together, the Substance Abuse and Mental Health Services Administration (SAMHSA), Indian Health Service (IHS), and the National Indian Health Board (NIHB) published a draft collaboratively written as The National Tribal Behavioral Health Agenda (NTBHA). This significant document expressed the profound reclamation of Tribal Nations' commitment to the long-lived eco-psychological attitude that is intrinsic to Indigenous and Aboriginal peoples by defining the essential necessity of these relationships in the promotion of individual and community mental health and wellness (Belton, 2016).

From the standpoint of the Indigenous Knowledge System (IKS), there is no separation between the health of the individual and the health of the community. The IKS embraces community as the entirety of the web of life that is the interconnected and interdependent beings alive on our shared home: this living planet. When we open to the awareness that the health of the planet is also the health of every other living being, we encounter the important concept of relationality and relational accountability.

The Indigenous scholar of the Cree Nation, Shawn Wilson (2008), reminds us that we know ourselves by our relationships and offers this thought:

> Identity for Indigenous peoples is grounded in their relationships with the land, with their ancestors who have returned to the land and with future generations who will come into being on the land. Rather than viewing ourselves as being in relationship with other people or things, we are the relationships that we hold and are part of. (p. 80)

Every human is indigenous to the planet. Every human has a story to tell about this relationship. The Indigenous and Aboriginal narratives are healing songs, stories, and dances co-created in balance, respect, and responsibility with nature. The promotion of community and individual health and mental wellness were often shared as personal tales, legends, or a sacred story in community with the intent to cultivate and ensure sustainability.

Indigenous scholar Gregory Cajete (2000) also described the eco-psychological attitude of relationality in his work, *Native Science: Natural Laws of Interdependence*, in this way:

> Key questions for traditional Native Americans included how individuals and the tribal community could ecologically respect the place in which they lived, and how a direct dialogue among the individual, the community and the natural world could be established and maintained.   Wherever Indigenous people lived they found a way to address these questions of survival and sustainability in profoundly elegant ways. They thought of their environment "richly" and in each

environment, they thought of themselves as truly alive and related. (p. 178)

Indigenous scholars Wilson and Cajete invite us to open up to the intrinsic nature of our inherent ecopsychological view, a vision as old as the Original and Aboriginal peoples on this planet, as well as a critical awareness that our relationality is intrinsic to the diverse expressions alive in an ethos of harmony. Consciously choosing to dwell in relationality invites one to open up to how other beings demonstrate a lived experience with nature and cultivates the eco-psychological attitude. Story and poetry are age-old portals of entry for examining our human experience with nature and one another, a threshold that has been documented through strata of diverse Indigenous and Aboriginal narratives from around the world, demonstrating the interdependent awareness of an ecopsychological attitude.

It has been said by non-Indigenous persons that when many think of ecopsychology, they think of the ocean and saving the environment. This position is a false sense of separation from our shared home, as an entity that is *over there*, some *thing* to be saved, ironically, by the very humans who contributed to the current dire conditions. This false sense of separation is indicative of subtle and overt remnants from a colonial past, continuing to thrive in the present as a "culture of conquest" (Dunbar-Ortiz, 2014) with calamitous consequences evident for our shared future. The Indigenous worldview invites us to examine that nature *is us* and clearly articulates the suffering of *all beings*.

In "A Gathering of Wisdoms," the Swinomish Mental Health Project (2002) described how the non-Native attitudes pertaining to a false sense of separation from nature, and therefore place, impact our mental health and well-being by disrupting the core of Indigenous spiritual values alive in the heart of interdependent awareness. The Swinomish Mental Health Project (2002) articulated the following:

> Most non-Indians did not, and still do not, have any appreciation for the multiplicity and subtle complexity of Indian spiritual systems. Indian spirituality pervades many aspects of Indian culture. For thousands of years it has provided Indian people with a deep contemplation of nature and the meaning of life and death and provide a set of socially

constructed values by which Indian people traditionally conduct their lives. (p. 40)

Exploring the ecopsychological may be new to most Western thinkers, but it is an ancient cosmology and code of ethical conduct for Indigenous peoples—an ethic whereby we are reminded that we are not a part of the environment or ecology, we *are* the living planet, *the ecology*. What is held between the pages of this anthology of poetry is an invitation. It is an invitation to re-member that which we have been dismembered from—our profound relationship to all of our relations, co-created in balance *with* Nature.

Nature and Existential Guilt

Existential psychologist Rollo May (1958) maintained that human nature can be understood in terms of one's connection with oneself, with other people, and with the physical world. Each of these realms includes possibilities or potentialities, but also the potential for *existential guilt*. Existential guilt is different from what May calls *normal guilt*. While normal guilt is the result of transgressions that one commits, existential guilt is rooted in human nature.

Existential guilt is a byproduct of one's limitations in conjunction with one's self-awareness. For example, when people do not live up to their potential, they may experience a type of existential guilt. Similarly, we may experience a type of existential guilt when we participate in an unjust system, even though we may not be able to avoid this.

May (1958) calls the existential guilt tied to the physical world "the most complex and comprehensive aspect" (p. 55) of existential guilt. It is also the one that is left the most unexplored (Hoffman, 2018). Hoffman notes that this form of existential guilt connects with environmental and ecological responsibility. In other words, one may experience existential guilt when one participates in activities that harm the environment or when one does not act to do more to protect or restore the environment. This guilt is existential in that it is something that one cannot completely prevent. Everyone does some harm to the environment, whether this involves driving a car, using harmful chemicals to clean, or not recycling when there is not a convenient recycling bin.

In today's world, it is easy to become overwhelmed by the number of important social and environmental causes that draw our attention.

It is not uncommon to hear about people driven to apathy because of this plethora of causes. But May (1958) points out that existential guilt includes a constructive potential. In other words, when one faces one's guilt directly, there is the potential to use it creatively and constructively. In this volume, one can see many examples of the creative and constructive use of existential guilt. If we are willing to look within by learning from outside ourselves, natural lessons are abundantly waiting to express their potential.

Reintegration

Much like a healthy relationship, nature is a mirror that can help us see ourselves more clearly through insight-giving opportunities. When trauma fragments our sense of self and strains our connection to self, to others, and to the world, nature can gather the pieces that remain of our assumptive world and assist us in regaining a sense of wholeness, meaning, and strength (see *Fireflies*). Through engagement and the openness (see *Selfscape*) of nature, we can return to a place of reintegration and synthesis formed through the modeling of nature's continual metamorphosis, as Muir (2018) wrote "out of one beautiful form into another" (Chapter 3, para. 31). However, there are environmental messages that can cause us to doubt our ability to be a part of, or belonging to, nature—such as being restricted to a setting that offers little opportunity to interact with nature (see *The Courtyard*). This includes the paradox of the potentially dangerous, yet healing, reality of nature (see *Volcano*) and one's acceptance of death through a fully engaging relationship with nature (*Father, when you call*).

For those who do not believe they understand poetry, I invite you to simply read with an open mind, open heart, and an open ear the experiences contained within. Many do not know the word *psithurism*, but they know what the wind blowing through the leaves of a tree sounds like. They may not know the word *petrichor*, but they recognize the very familiar smell of the earth after a rain. Allow your experiences to open your heart as way to listen to the authors of these works, and the reader may just be surprised at how connected we are, even if the content of our experiences is different. The beauty in this is that the shared voices in this anthology span race, gender, age, and nationality. This work contains authors from India, Canada, Zimbabwe, Australia, and all across the United States. Through a shared love for nature, our expressions arise because nature has modeled its acceptance of interconnectedness and interdependency in a manner that has brought voices from around the world into this body of work.

Perhaps when we listen with our heart, all of our world will be closer and will feel more connected through our grounding to each other and nature. Will you take a walk with us?

References

Belton, G. (2016). *Soror mystica wears a red dress in our last wild place.* Unpublished dissertation. Santa Barbara, CA: Pacifica Graduate Institute.

Cajete, G. (2000). *Native science: Natural laws of interdependence.* Santa Fe, NM: Clear Light.

Dunbar-Ortiz, R. (2014). *An Indigenous people's history of the United States.* Boston, MA: Beacon Press.

Hillman, J. (2017). *The soul's code: In search of character and calling.* New York, NY: Ballantine Books.

Hoffman, L. (2018). Existential guilt. In D. Leeming (Ed.), *The encyclopedia of psychology and religion* (3rd ed.). Advance online publication. Berlin, Germany: Springer. https://doi.org/10.1007/978-3-642-27771-9_200194-1

May, R. (1958). Contributions of existential psychotherapy. In R. May, E. Angel, & H. F. Ellenberger (Eds.), *Existence* (pp. 37–91). Northvale, NJ: Jason Aronson.

Muir, J. (2018). *Our national parks* [Kindle Version]. Vertebrate Digital. Retrieved from www.amazon.com.

Swinomish Tribal Community (2002). *A gathering of wisdoms: Tribal mental health, a cultural perspective.* LaConner, WA: Swinomish Tribal Community.

Wilson, S. (2008). *Research is ceremony: Indigenous research methods.* Winnipeg, Canada: Fernwood.

Poems

Be Like a River

Gina Subia Belton

River meditation
Calls for the Soul of woman
Unfolding in turns

Scars of Terra

Derrick Sebree, Jr.

Scars of terra
Earthly fissures
Churning, moving

Through fiery resistance

Balancing pain with love
Blood of my ancestors
Coloring the Earth

Tears of the Earth
Carried on breath
Nourish the body

Feed the soul

Transform the land
Love my ancestors

Alone and Detached
Michael Moats

Alone and detached.
Presenting a final show.
Appreciation.

Photograph "Final Show" by Michael Moats

Desert Dweller

Cynthia Anderson

Don't listen to what anyone says—

if you want to be baptized
in the place of no water,

humans are not the center.
Arrive on a lenticular cloud,

chart the maze of sand and rock—

let heat flay your flimsy skin,
expose your core to light.

No grief is too great
for this wilderness to devour,

no anger too vast, if you muster
the courage to stay,

find your own way
to be an eremite—

The desert has died and come back
ten thousand times and will not

let you forget—every last creature
inhabits you, part of you.

Follow the trail to the end
and keep going—

your ears will fill with music.
Dig in when the earth starts

to shake, when flood, fire, and gale
remake your chosen ground—

if your heart's not in it,
you won't be here long.

***

"Desert Dweller" was previously published in *Desert Dweller* by Cynthia
Anderson. Published by Pencil Cholla Press, 2014.

The Seduction of Winter

Alison Johnson

This is, I know, the winter of life.
I gave up the vegetable garden when I sold the house.
Seedling starts in March, by July morning cucumber harvest.
And in the fall, slow cooking tomatoes for winter meals.

Now I plant a few flowers.
Is this life's sum?
Raising flowers?

I stand over the sink, peeling and eating an orange,
looking out over the late summer prairie lands.
The fox steps out.
I have seen her before,
we live in deliberate and intimate proximity.
Her home the prairie, steps from my small home,
methodically ordered for life's winter.
Confident and poised (she not I)
She skirts the house, retires to the prairie.

I pick the seeds from the orange and think –
Perhaps they will sprout.

Grief

Jason Dias

Outside, pine trees reach
Achingly towards the snow
Falling from frigid heights.
Clusters of pine cones grasp
For snowy Earth like
Finger-shaped bananas.
None of your neon greens or
Delicious yellows here:
Only nutty beige,
Hostile thorns,
Closed-up cones.
Atop the branches, a thick
Layer of soft winter snow,
Gentle to the touch but bitingly cold,
Comforting and killing.
This tree is an aged crone,
Dying and giving birth at once,
And in her own labor is reborn.

***

"Grief" was previously published in *Violet Haze* by Jason Dias. Published by Superluminal Velocity Books, 2017.

Renewal

Autumn J. Patz

Ground crumbled beneath my feet
and I plummeted
faster towards Earth's core.
Arms failing, reaching
to grab onto something,
but no roots aided.

Temperature rising,
wind rushing,
breath shortening,
anxiety heightening.

Splash—
fiery lakes engulfed me,
devouring skin,
devastating bones,
demolishing heart,
digesting soul,
nothing remained except a seedling—
my sunflower phoenix ready
to reach the sun.

Beauty is best born from havoc.

Listening to Bees
Heidi Elizabeth Blankenship

How do we fix all the things that are broken?
I'm not asking about window screens
or bathroom doors
or flat tires.
How do we fix
important things
like broken hearts
cracked into
aching chasms,
or an argument with your mother
the week before she dies,
or the moment requiring
more words or less,
or maybe an action—
too late?
The bees in my yard
land on the lips
of the red aloe flowers
and crawl in
head first,
disappearing completely
within those hollow
ruby walls,
then emerging again,
as though re-birthed.
Perhaps that is the way
of things,
crawling deep inside
a beautiful space,
extracting all
there is to know,
then re-emerging.

Haibun for Crows
Andrena Zawinski

...whose fiery eyes now burned into my bosom's core—Poe

Two crows fix eyes on me. Flapping, they twitter, rattle,
and click unlike yesterday's loosening of brash caws
as I first passed under their tree, the pine where now
a dead one lies belly down and beak up. The murder descends,
mobbing as if to decide some fate in cackles and chirps.
Then as suddenly as landing, they lift off—
                              span the open sky
                              in thick branches of black sheen
                              crisscrossing clear blue

The Doe
Dana Sonnenschein

In the midnight yard
you can see only moonlit snow,
        tree trunks and shadows,
the wind shifting branches,
        and then you hear deliberate steps
                and a sudden staccato
of crunch and silence, a leaping
        that could be anything—
unless you recognize the cadence
        of hesitation and confidence,
                the way deer hooves cut
through light snow, frozen sleet,
        last fall's oak and hickory leaves.

From season to season, deer move
        like thoughts, finding their way
in light and darkness. I've watched them
        in the early morning and at twilight
following one another up the hill,
        their legs fine as saplings,
                brown backs angled this way and that,
                        ears flickering like leaves;
I've seen the occasional spikehorn
        and a buck with antlers branching,
standing, fearless in the sunlit garden
        where he'd nipped the newest green
                and every last purple tulip.

I've found the hosta border browsed,
        plans and plantings crushed,
                pumpkins broken for their seeds,
so I know what moves,
        fleet and sure among the trees,
sounding larger in the dark yet less material.
        Whatever I fear, that rustling
and snapping is not the past or future
        creeping up on me;

it's not something with sharp teeth and claws
but one of many slim-ankled whitetails
        who haunt the nearby woods and fields
                and sleep beneath pines when it snows.

Once, still as stumps, in a storm-wrecked
        November forest, my lover and I
watched a startled doe bound away
        from walkers and talkers on the path,
                away from the brook, away from the lake,
across the hill and at us, hurtling
        ahead of the sound of her feet,
                taller and heavier than we thought
a deer could be, and she turned aside
        about fifteen feet from where we stood,
                caught between awe and joy,
and we could breathe again.
        I've been listening for her ever since.

Seeds of the Sacred

Richard Bargdill

An ancient voice echoes through the house
As if a hybrid of dogs and coyotes howl
In celebration of traditions gone
Of weaving and seeing the moon
And the loon in the lake
Recognizing the importance of
The land and the water
And the bees and the seas
And the Seeds.

An ancient voice that may have come
Through a divining rod
Planted deep in the heart of a
Crack in the concrete
Where a weed might have grown
Or the pains of a people propagated enough so
That the bones and the dust of our Ancestors—
Dust living on a larger Dust—
Blown by the wind
Floating on the seas as they rise
Climbing up and pulling down upon
Wave and vibe and light and land.

Sometimes you can still see it
In the eyes of an Ancient one
The Ones wondering alone—
Not staring into phones—
Those whose task it is to ask
How refined minds can be further opened
Those somehow still on a pilgrimage
On a quest to find what remains
Of the sacred, remains of the vital:
The final seeds.

And oddly enough
Those seeds might just be stored
In a single room

That allows the sound
To echo just so
Like the Ancient soul
Of this old
  Voice.

Rainy Day Charm
Ann Christine Tabaka

A rainy day falls from the sky.
Bare feet splash in puddles.
Cloud-filtered light imparts a
dreamy glow. The feeling of
motionless time invades reality.

Inside stillness,
listening to the sounds soft rain
makes. Melodic trickling transfixes
the mind. A lazy yawn emanates,
permeating the silence.

Outside, small rivulets form,
carrying dried-leaf boats out
to swirling miniature seas.
Teasing the imagination,
stories unfold.

Bright azure patches peek
through an overcast sky, wishing
for a rainbow. Rainy day charm wanes
as the day lapses into evening, and a
soggy world closes its eyes once more.

Elemental Yoga

Anne Ness

I sink into the floor, it becomes loam and sand and rock,
Cradling me in Earth energy. Mother Earth envelopes and enters,
She in me and me in her, making my bones strong
And my muscles thick. I thank her.
I rise and inhale the sweet perfume of Mother Air.
My lungs expand with joy and breathe out into the world.
Thank you, Mother Air, Goddess of the rising sun.
I salivate to the West and feel the rising tide of water within
And thank you, Mother of Water, Oshun, beloved.
I breathe rapidly out, pulling in my core, quickly, and relax.
Twenty-seven times, and again and again.
Fire rises and my body is energized.
Thank you, Hestia, Gabija, Vesta, Pele.
I pray for an end to suffering for all people.
I am balanced. In and out,
up and down,
all around.
Energy is my Goddesses' blessing.
Let me be a small channel of your magnificence.

November Tree

C. Richard Patton

Mid-November and a tree
stands alone,
in the rough between what will be a YMCA
and what almost is a savings bank.
But today the tree stands alone,
a hundred feet from anything
made by man and it doesn't care.
Nor do I at the moment.
There is no weather here, now;
the air is calm but not dead,
the sky has a high haze;
though it is mid-morning
there is no visible sun,
no light and shade.
It's not overcast
in any noticeable way,
no oppressant cloud base.
In my full sleeves and pants I
am not cool (much less cold) and I
am not warm (much less hot).
No leaves fall.
No people pass.
A tree stands alone.

Pulchritude

Ben Shank

You shrug off your lingerie of snow
to better switch whip
the pale haunches of that tawdry sun of winter.

You sarong yourself
with the full pulchritude of summer
turning so frowsy and green
you make me scoff at the probability of winter
even as I miss your naked limbs.

You stand sentinel
over my days and nights
never costing me a nickel.

Oh, lucky me
born in the nick of time
to bear witness to you
making adroit majesty
look easy.

The Elders
Elizabeth Tornes

They are still with us,
waving as oak leaves, roaring
wind through the pines. They echo
as woodpeckers hammering
hollow trees. They insist
that we remember, remember,
remember their stories
and their long-lived lives.
Remember the hand
they gave us when we slipped,
the kind looks and words,
a balm for soothing a heartache.

I miss the grandmothers
who gentled me, who taught me
how to speak, and give to others.
How to go beyond the self
to hear the pulse of barred owls
signifying wisdom,
the high-pitched songs of frogs
that lift the swamp
in the early evening,
the loon's tremulous call--
the voice of the Creator,
if we would only listen.

***

"The Elders" was originally published in the *Wisconsin Fellowship of Poets Poetry Quilt*, 2016.

Equine Connections

Bev Lyles

I come to you and you receive me.
We meet not just forehead to forehead, or heart to heart,
But as enveloping spirits.
Others say I am a hole—with nothing inside;
You say I am whole—just the way I was made.
Everything I have done, I've done alone—
No one believed me capable or deserving—
But can I go on alone?
Life spits at me, undermining every step like a rising tide;
People make fun—they believe we are not real—and go on their way.
I am designated to the outside, looking in.
Yet who is blessed but the natural one?
The one who feels the ways of the earth; who lives within their
nature—
Never questioning, because there is no other answer.
It is better to know my self and be with you in a world gone crazy.
Because we are connected, we have outlived all.
And so, we walk on!

The Homes of Birds
Brook Bhagat

I understand the funeral I have
the address the dress the time

It begins with smiling cameras
and ends with paper tablecloths
deviled eggs and cold cuts downstairs I
understand but it
doesn't feel right
none of it

the worst part is the day outside
with its sunshine all those
empty minutes left and I think
I would have lost it if not

for the hike, still in our black together,
you and Ben, the boy,
me and my sister arm in arm
down the easy path at
Garden of the Gods,

lighter than before, noticing the homes
of birds in the rocks and remembering
we are just a moment, fragments
of a mystery that flies and sings.

Vigil Keeping
Candace Hennekens

Strong south winds shake bare trees
in the front yard, making them dance, sway.
Sometimes weather like this brings
a flock of robins, returning barn swallows.
My husband is dying. He's slept all day.
My sister telephoned this morning.
Maybe he will go today is what she said,
speaking of the wind, what it could take.

As the sunset lengthens, spreading pink,
I sit by the front window. I've been expecting
that he will sit up, say hello, and ask
"What's for dinner?"
I realize now, this isn't going to happen.
Gone those days. Instead more medicine,
smiles, and then closed eyes once again.
I sit to watch as pink turns gray,
as wind continues, even though
sun is now gone. Soon I will rise,
make my dinner, eat alone,
keeping vigil, listening to the furnace burn oil,
and take from this time anything it offers,
wind, quiet peace of house, his sweet slumber,
another day to be with him, even intense sadness
that transforms swaying trees and bushes
into a sort of whirling dervish prayer.

***

"Vigil Keeping" was originally published in the *Ariel Anthology* by Wisconsin Fellowship of Poets (Author) and Deanna Yost (Editor), 2017.

Good Morning
Kai Siedenburg

The birds
sound
like I
feel—

thrilled
to behold
the everyday
miracle

of another
sunrise;

eager
to discover
what gifts
the morning
will bring.

Together,
we welcome
the new day.

My heart sings
and flies
with them.

***

"Good Morning" was originally published in *Poems of Earth and Spirit: 70 Poems and 40 Practices to Deepen Your Connection with Nature* by Kai Siedenburg. Published by Our Nature Connection, 2017.

Larkspur Trail
Carol Barrett

Pine boughs nod their whisking *yes*
to this noble exercise of heart
and song, this wind-swept walk along

a foaming creek that pulls north
like a drunken river, the walkers' arms
latched to torsos, ambling in rhythm,

hands hooked in loose seam, heads
cocked to the rush of water over wet
slate. A child in plaid skirt skips ahead

like a small stone tossed from the wrist.
A spaniel heads their way, bounding
beyond his master, pulling, intent

on covering the sun-smoked turf
before the sky can shift gears, settle
the doves in rafters, the quail in coveys

among the sage. The dog is happy
as the smell of barbecues
drifts through cedar slats. He makes

the walkers' faces light. When they began,
they did not know any of this:
girl, dog, bird, pine, stream. Only

that the body needs its ground,
its holy place in the fine dust of things.
Larkspur nesting, they won't tell where.

***

"Larkspur Trail" was originally published in *Crosswinds Poetry Journal*, 2016.

Of Sky and Earth #28 *by Stephen Linsteadt*

No / Igneous Boundary
Cindy Rinne

I scale down thick granitic magma, touch the molten past of violent eruptions, and sense the pulse. Then I descend beyond split boulders. Lean back to catch my balance. The flow of blotched stone pours down the mountainside. There is no edge. I go farther. No place to look straight down. I scale farther. No / igneous boundary. I halt. Nearby, an ancient tree trunk watches lizards bounce and the manzanita sway. I thank the barren rock and the tree's shadow for a place to sit. Faint mineral layers absorb me— quartz, feldspar, and rough mica. Above, the pock-marked horizon looms like a message on papyrus. Two people in muffled conversation turn and walk away. A beetle like a winged scarab comes close. I chase it. Beyond, branches yield like shed antlers, bleached bones. Wind gusts soar and outline my face.

Old Man
Stephen Schwei

The old man rests his feet
on the raised-up root
of an October willow.
He bends down,
retrieves a discarded cap
and dangles it off the lowest limb,
not knowing that its owner
hung himself in these woods,
never will return to notice
the thoughtful gentleness
of age and autumn.

Perhaps the old man's wife
hung herself years ago.
They had been divorced.
All he got was a call from the east
informing of suicide, explaining
that no one could lend him the money
to make the trip to the funeral.
So he lit a candle
and gathered up money
to send flowers to a memory.

Standing here years later
deciding the rocks
are too full of moss
for an old man to take off his shoes
and balance to the other bank
to get closer to the two sparrows
dipping in the water and
flying to the vacant stump.

There's really no reason this cap
should lie here in the mud.

The Walk

Ted Bowman

The walk was with her through forest and fields.
Autumn filled nostrils,
Horses to the left, sheep to the right.
We stepped on stones to cross streams,
Over fence gates and fallen trees,
Surrounded by bleats, neighs and caws,
Crunching and conversation,
All competing for attention

It was exactly
What he and I would have loved to do
It had become our ritual
An almost annual rite to walk and talk
The noble Englishman
And his American companion
Rarely a dog, only we two

For over two years now
He has walked uphill into Parkinson's
Stepping on uneven ground
Grief on the one side, hope on the other
Tests and procedures leading to ambiguity
Just over the next hill
None of it as attractive as sunsets in autumn

I'm glad she and I walked
It was our first
Not to be our last
Somehow it seemed a salute
To him and our score-long ritual
Walking with him is irreplaceable
Walking is indispensable
I'm glad the three of us did it

Back to Jackfork Quarry

Stacy Pendergrast

>   open blinds —
>   in moonlight I give
>   words to my secret

Now that we're married, at night, under the covers, I spit out the story, what happened decades ago. You say you remember that swimming hole. It was by the army base. You swam there, back in the day.

"Probably shut down now," you say. You fluff the pillow, pull me into our spoon position and whisper, "I would have kicked their asses."

"I have to find that place," I say.

"I'll go with you."

A few days later, we take a drive, following the GPS coordinates to the area shown by the blue splotch on my cellphone screen. At Camp Robinson the armed guard says, "You can't get there from here."

On the other side of the mountain, we park near the repair shop. The neon sign glows with the word TIRES. Across the highway, NO TRESPASSING flaps near a rusted gate.

>   off-trail —
>   instead of my compass
>   I follow you

Within minutes into woods thick with vetches and thorny vines, I'm wondering if this is a bad idea.

"It's just half a mile," you say.

As we climb, I hear only the crack of branches and leaves. In the first clearing, we stumble onto an ATV trail that cuts across the mountain. I sink into the muddy tracks and think of the teenage guys, one with the beard of a man, who'd brought me here when I was thirteen. *You mean you got in a car with five strange boys?* my girlfriend asked when I recently told her, practice for telling you.

"Shh . . . What's that noise?" I ask and look behind.

>   distant dog   barks day into   dusk

"Let's forget it," I say. I check my cell phone to see if we've lost reception. Then I stick two crossed branches into tire tracks, a breadcrumb sign.

"We're almost there." We enter another thicket of trees, and just as I'm about to beg to turn back — you exclaim, "Here it is!"

The forest opens into a gorge. Its water is a luminous shade of blue — Picture the color of a robin's egg melted into liquid, then add shimmer. This is the place I remember — with its pine branches, hung like lace canopies. There is the rock slab where they each took a turn, first pounding his chest, then diving into the pool, as I waited in the shade, my fingers curled into themselves.

> sky deepening
> its blue in
> a wallow

Only in the stillness of water and wood, I am grounded enough to watch my girl-self in the scene I've replayed: *Pinned under pines, my glasses gone, the trees a blurry mass of green. Hands yank and bruise. Bone on bone, knuckles and knees. I give up trying, my tears pop like bullets — And then, after they strip me of my pants and underwear . . . they stop.* There is nothing more to tell, but still a secret to keep, for all these years.

"This is so beautiful," you say as you lean over the ledge, your cell camera snatching pieces of green and blue.

> clouds mirrored
> in quarry pool —
> close as I can get to sky

"It's a wonder I'm here," I say and drop a rock from the ledge.

> stillness lengthening
> the stone's ripples —
> that mistake from childhood

We scoop pebbles. They practically sparkle. I'd read that miners found crystals in the sandstone here.

skipping   pond rocks   the memories   we keep

    We don't see any of our trail markings on the way back, but we don't need them.

> trail's end—
> I give the pebble in my shoe
>   back to the mountain

***

"Back to Jackfork Quarry" was originally published in *Memoir Magazine*. Published by Memoir Magazine, LLC, August 2019.

Suspension
Toti O'Brien

Now the majesty
of a barren tree
cut against the pale sky
lifts her sorrow
as the flight of myriads
of sparrows does.

Some of them
perch on branches.
Some press
diminutive feet
against the trunk's
vertical surface.

They hang
perpendicular
uncaring of gravity.
Their suspended pose
is so improbable
it puzzles her mind.

But isn't her stance
as unlikely as theirs?
To sit on this lawn
inhabit this corner of time.
To witness these sparrows
this tree.

Breath by Breath
Elaine Reardon

Is it wrong to avoid thinking,
listening to Moss Brook slosh over stones?
To notice the black crickets dart between
blades of dry grass and goldenrod,
time tellers of the changing season?

I wanted only to remember Jenny
as she sat on the largest rock midstream,
legs tucked, reading a book,
as the brook rushed by.

And now I learn to meditate, to take
one breath at a time, to notice
my ribs rise and fall, to notice the air
fill me, leave, time and time again.

Some say *the only moment is now,*
all is illusory, breathe through pain.
There is some comfort in this
moment by moment, breath by breath.

Opening
Eric Windhorst

Gliding on glass
The wooden sword in my hand
slices through the surface
My canoe
leaves a wound
on her face

Gently,
waves start to rock my vessel
I pause—
holding my oar still

Suddenly,
my veil is torn
Nothing separates me
from her healing embrace

Mountains holding this sea inside
her life
our life

I close my eyes
and drink in the morning

Asking the Birds
Carol L. Deering

for sustenance
like a willow fingering
the breeze,
a stone willing itself
to bloom in the draw,
a cloud of spider lace
snagging the trees,
my wrist

exchanging its talent
as a bridge
for an open cup of twigs,
a modest space
crafted of mud, shade,
and the jittery need
to generate
and rest.

Penciled Sunlight

Diane Hovey

Each day of my daily planner
I penciled in sunlight.
Year after year, I did the same
knowing this was the elixir
upon which my life depended.
Yet, I penciled it in,
gave it the option to be
erased,
and I did, year after year,
to make room
for other shouting demands
and could not understand
why,
why I no longer had the
energy to walk out the door
with my soul purpose
to soak in the sun.

This year, I resolve to use ink.

How Love Shows Up
Kathy O'Fallon

Happy's sleeping at my feet
when the neighbor dog's serenade
woos me from the screen.
I open the door, climb back in bed,
shaking my head. I still can't resist
a crooner. My dog scoots
his way to my rear and Bear sidles up
to the headboard, *his* butt now within reach,
tells me in his Chewbacca voice
he could use a scratch just above the hip
(an itch that's been plaguing him for weeks).
Happy repositions for a belly massage,
and then the bath begins. His tongue strokes
my arm like a man in heat, works its way up
to the delicious face cream,
but what he really means is:
get your lazy ass out of bed
for our car ride to the river for a dip.

The dogs run ahead, I take my time
in the shadows, oak leaves now beginning
to adorn and adore me, thanks to a quiet
October breeze. A certain mosquito
finds me mouthwatering, and the crows'
enthusiasm at my arrival sounds almost apoplectic—
their upper-west-side accent the only snooty thing
about them. Then there's my arthritis
that won't leave me for a second,
wrapping itself around my fingers
like a fuzzy blanket. And I'm almost embarrassed
to mention the blood moon romancing me 24/7—
even lovers need a time out to resuscitate.
And I can't forget the garbage truck
I almost hit on our way,
that big-bellied Greek charmer
backing *its* butt up my driveway,
getting me all flustered—cradles and swallows

whatever I've discarded,
like a husband who takes his vows seriously.

Taps
Joan Wiese Johannes

It is syrup time,
and Tom tramps, taps, and talks
about the bear who took ten buckets
and left tracks around his camp.
He shakes his head and says
he hopes the fire
keeps it away when he boils down,
tells me he applied for a permit
as he mimes the pull of a trigger.

But I like his bear
will follow the trail of white buckets,
drink sap clear as streams.

I plan to walk circles around spring
before the big boil-down turns me
dark as bear fur thick as blood.

***

"Taps" was originally published in *Peninsula Pulse*, August 2005; also
published in *Sensible Shoes* by Joan Wiese Johannes. Published by New
Dawn Unlimited, 2010.

The Triple Duck

Larry Blazek

you and a friend go fishing
in an old wooden john boat
upon a long, narrow pond
your tackle is a kite string
wrapped around a short stick
and a large fish hook
you companion rows around the pond
you keep casting
you hook something
it gets loose
then you hook it again
much to your surprise
instead of a fish
you pull in a small white duck
with three heads
you dislodge the hook carefully
tuck the duck under your arm
you companion retrieves
a cardboard box
from a handy refuse bin
you plan to delay the execution
of the duck until it fattens up

Illusion in Blue

Leonore Hildebrandt

Lately, our tenses are neither
present nor past, but impossibly
absent as we try to take hold.

Contrary to what is written, you say,
the birds in the sky always
hustle for sustenance.
The fish in the sea
worry themselves dull
over tomorrow's catch.

The rush is contagious—
I had to omit the pauses between
breathing in and breathing out.
It is winter—we don't sleep—
we roam about the dark
in search of kernels.

Today, as the snow is receding,
brown grasses are laid out
to dry in the sun:
the thin carpet of life
a single line. I close my eyes
—blue water, blue sky—

and launch myself deep
in the light-world.
You come too.

***

"Illusion in Blue" was originally published in *Otis Nebula*. Published by Otis Nebula Press, Winter 2012.

Analog Walk

Nancy K. Jentsch

On an analog walk
no thumbs drum
no earbuds pulse
no Fitbits tick

but champagne breeze prickles skin
birdsong bounces between wires
the bend ahead promises Oz
musky smells and sapsucker tapping
braid with the shade of a stand of trees

Deer's stare
salamander's surprise
freeze time
so that
now
gains depth and breath
to sustain beyond
drumming pulsing ticking
at walk's end

The Uncertainty of Snow
Scott Seward

A frozen ocean of heavy, slushy-white snow,
Lies patiently out in front of me, waiting,
Its crushing mass underneath, yet,
Atop...its thin diamond hard
Skin of refractive luminosity,
Sparkles like a bedazzled
Crown of jewels...
It's ostensibly crystalline,
A kaleidoscopic novelty,
That Sings a Windy Song with
A fierce snowy breeze...
Something so pure and beautiful
Filled with such blind impermanence
Will have you crying one day... please.

What a wonderful puzzle we humans are,
With our most exquisite and divine regret,
With so many of us, we must learn,
The Golden Art of...how to learn...how to forget.
I see the cotton-candy-blue shadows
Sprayed out across, white, wispy snow, so
Nature could paint Her patent display of
Periwinkle hue into Nature's fractals,
Shapes and shadows intertwine into
A new Line of counterpoint and interplay.
The crispy crusts of snowy crystalline,
A Shiny new face of a four-of-a-kind
Milky Way stars bathe us in Milky Way shine,
Against the inky blackness of the
Nighttime sky and the powder blue Earth
Weaves into a brilliant disguise.

Beneath the slow Zen commotion,
There is a hazy notion,
Locked away, so wise, that
Enemies of Truth
And Love will despise,

So the rest of us must learn to Realize:
Love is the polar opposite of fear.
And yet this charcoal grey world
Can be humanely civilized, even colorized,
And hypnotized, so that it will see
What is truth and what is clear,
What is a fact, and what is a fantasy?

And again, Winter gives way to Spring,
As Summer to Fall is quite another thing
But we should all recall the circular ring
That binds us to this universe fling
And within it, the beginning of everything.
Space time magic floating in a plasma sea
Heisenberg's Rule of Uncertainty.
The beauty lies within the
Interconnectedness
Of everything,
And uncertainty.

The Easterlies
Evin Phoenix

When the waters rush with heavy tides
And in one moment, all is lost
The flood, which fills the cracks inside
But leaves my open lips unwashed

Consuming all, the Earth and sea
The power of a primal force
One dares not argue with gravity
Nor the nature of a torrent's source

But if my navigation fails me
If I lose my compass rose
If my sextant falls into the sea
My vessel, nearing rocks exposed

Then I steer yet ever onward
To the skies beyond the storm
Leaving battle scars of bloody shores
Laid to waste from squalls before

For the Easterlies have brought anew
Stillness, on the pink skyline
I know that's where my ship is due —
To the waters of a gentler shoreline

True Nature

Don Hardison

I found the forest inside myself
And for the sake of love
Never cut a limb, branch, or trunk

Instead I sat, and sunk
Deep between roots and dust,
Bugs and funk
Breathing like a Buddhist monk
I came to peace

Intoxicating Songs and Sights
Ndaba Sibanda

I just like to stray into the forest each time l visit the countryside
How I like to immerse myself into its thickness and feel the
awesomeness of Mother Nature surge into my veins

The proximity to a life undiluted intoxicates my spirits
I heed the birds' advice as they sing their happy
harmonies in their charming and chirping ways

Their serenading expertly makes love to my eardrums
I can't tell you how the creepy reptiles wow me
to no end as they wiggle and jiggle in their
amazing fashion to their hazy habitats

I marvel at the beauty of vegetation
and condemn deforestation
in the strongest possible
terms

***

"Intoxicating Songs and Sights" was originally published in *Whispers*, September 2013; also published in *The News Chronicle*, November, 2013; published in *Piker Press*, August 2014; also published in NonDoc, January 2017; also published in *The Song Is...* by Marianne Szlyk, and received an honorable mention in a contest for Thelma's Prize. Published by *The Song Is...*, July 2017; also published in *Journal of Artistic Creation and Literary Research*, published by Universidad Complutense de Madrid, January 2018.

Fireflies

Sharon K. Sheppard

Among the tall grasses
dampened by rain,
along the pale pink pathways
of waning light
spark-like, they flare
then fade. O to wander
where fireflies rise,
to float out
over this bristling world,
and pour into it
a little light
then fade unafraid
into night
and have that be
enough.

***

"Fireflies" was originally published in *To Imagine a* Life by Sharon K. Sheppard. Published by Sharon Sheppard, 2017.

Because the Finches

Diane Elayne Dees

Because the finches have arrived
to deliver their gifts of gold and red—
despite these days of grief and dread,
I suddenly feel more alive.

How easily the finches thrive;
they sing while waiting to be fed.
Then, sated with niger, they survive
to deliver more gifts of gold and red,

while I still struggle to contrive
a reason to get out of bed.
It's dark and bleak inside my head,
but for a moment, I'm revived
because the finches have arrived.

The Existence that Shapes Us

Emily Lasinsky

My heart is heavy
for the people of the world.
I know there's love,
but I don't know how much it catches,
or intentionally weaves
where leaves depart because they know
it's coming...
the wind that bends and
shapes branches and bones.

Common as Grass *by Richard Bargdill*

Windfall

Hilary Leighton

Fallen from an ancient cottonwood a broken branch waits
A broken branch patiently waits while tiny creatures find
nourishment in her bark
Creatures find her nourishing and the old branch is made holey
The old branch is made holy as winds blow right through her
Wild winds blow soft hymns
Hymns from the wild are songs of the earth
Wild earth songs are ancient prayers sung through broken branches
Ancient branches break, fall, pray and sing

Solar Storm
Whitney Scott

Our earth spins daily, wobbling on its axis
as each year it revolves in steady orbit, a great blue mass
around the sun, that flaming star, which can erupt.
Then a solar flare, rare, flames out for miles then rains back down,
a plasma storm enfolded in upon itself,
a burnt char cloud enshrouding half its host.

Seasons turn with revolution, and fascinate.
Grateful for the greening buds
and turning leaves whose orange reds return to earth,
all my cells smile up at Brother Sun, gold on my birch trio
that nod and sway, greeting me, and I, them;
quartet in motion, we breathe in concert with the solar light.

My Sister Moon pulls my inner tides,
has me loving her through window panes
still warm from summer's solar heat,
and in winter, through sharp arrays of frost on glass—
just as she tugs at roughly textured trees that stretch,
seek to touch her paleness in the sky with waving branches.

Those who feel our inner tango, our pulsing beat,
can listen to the journey of the moon, unending,
marvel at the rhythms of the dancing trees
as moons turn my tides; find remedies for dreams denied.
So when I reach for Sun, flaming, baked and purifying,
Moon soon reaches back, cooling in her silver light, and calming.

Faith in Us

Jeffrey Johannes

Sometimes I choose
a spot on a quiet page
and write down
something unusual
such as the story of
how everyone
on a street
in Chinatown
walked carefully
while a woman chased
hundreds of tiny turtles
after they got loose
from a tank
in her market stall.
Not one turtle
was harmed.
And this mercy
lifts my spirits,
reminds me that
acts of kindness
appear like moths
circling our porch lights
drawn to the light.

***

"Faith in Us" was previously published in *The Best of Kindness: Origami Poems* by Jan Keough and Kevin Keough (Editor). Origami Poems Project, 2016.

Oak Tree
Joan Moritz

I am like the oak which will not shed its leaves,
holding tight to autumn's curled brown crusts
although they shudder in the winter wind
and slowly fill with snow. They need to go,

I know. I need to clear a place for growth
and greening buds. It's time to once again
believe that life will surely follow death,
for this is nature's constant song, her finest gift.

Outlandish Orchid

Maria Elena B. Mahler

A single stem rushes
into the air, bursting inside

my kitchen window.
The purple petals peek

and smile at me every morning
like a child to her mother,

unconcerned with her place
in this world.

Far from tropical rain falling
on green canopy, uprooted

from the trunk of a palm
or a banyan tree,

she breathes in tap water,
while I scrub pans.

She blooms year after year,
not a tear rolls down her cheek.

Returning Nature's Favor
Marilyn Zelke Windau

Silently your leaves fall to the forest floor.
Loudly your raindrops pellet the earth.
You give us favor.

You honor your dead,
blessing them with snow cover—
the highway-sacrificed deer,
who seek the sanctuary of the wood to die,
the foxes, skunks, opossums,
the old, the babies,
the myriad of butterflies, moths, and beetles.
You welcome their bodies' gifts.

You gather bouquets: purple asters of fall,
marsh marigolds of spring,
wild sage and feather fern of summer,
wintergreen with their crimson drop beads,
blue gentian trumpeting their glory near streams.

You call on your helpers, the worms,
the microbe armies, the heat of sun
to help you create anew.

Time is not in minutes for you.
Time is not in hours.
Time is days, weeks, months,
years of wait, and weight
of leaves, of flowers, of insects,
of layers of life.

All will come forth again, nurtured.

We, as humans, can only return that favor.
We can help.
We can aid you with our efforts.
We can put together substances.
We can honor your soils.

Pear Trees on Irving Street

Richard Widerkehr

They float, these white trees--
a few petals, fallen
to the street, not stars fading,
not snow.

The trees have blossomed
in a freezing east wind.
None, I think, has any regrets
or choice.

If the night frost
comes too thick,
too fast, they'll give
what they have to,

as if it were nothing--
these clusters,
held not by black branches,
but their own buoyancy.

***

"Pear Trees on Irving Street" was originally published in *Gravel*, April 2016;
also published in *Presence of Absence* by Richard Widerkehr (Author) and
Lana Ayers (Editor). Published by MoonPath Press, 2017.

It Won't Stop Being Gorgeous Outside
Julie Ann Wenglinski

No vain rose,
I cover my bruises and bites
with long clothes
and dig and divide the bed again.

Ignoring my stabbing back,
I hack at clumps of liriope
and pull out their broken roots
like a mammoth's tooth.

A grassy breeze from my youth
brushes by me.
I stand and lick the salt from my lip,
stretch and forget the pain.

This time is spent
overlooking black spots
and painting the empty spaces
of my new page with blooms.

My Own Space

Joe Amaral

I scoop and shovel,
taking anxious glances
out vast ocean

where my dark wedge
horizons the waterline–
staining the sultry blue.

Hastily, I fill
colorful pails,
placing them in my kayak.

I row and grunt, adding sand
to the mound to create
my own island. I install

palm trees for shade,
humming in shirtless isolation
with pitter-patter waves.

Soon, I hear heavy breathing
and laughter. Engines scythe
the serene tidal wisp

as party boats crash my solitude.
Undiscovered no longer, I
find myself back where I started,

clopping the smooth-topped seas.
I dig and rebuild all over again,
oars searching for peace.

I will not shrink from this world.

I will expand open space.

Walk

Heather Wyatt

I take a walk
with my dog
on a familiar path
behind a school
near my home.
We are going faster
than I would like
as my Labrador mix
with a tiny head
races for nothing.

There are still patches
of green because the winter
is mild.
I don't wear a jacket.

The street seems old,
with imperfections
and the trees ignore
us on our path.

My dog stops
to lift his leg
and the thought
crosses my mind
that this is far less poetic
than stopping by woods
on a snowy evening
or not stopping for death
before it kindly stops for me.

I cross the road
and as usual
the dog pauses
on the yellow lines,
waiting for me
to tug his leash

or tell a silly joke.

Slipping behind a fence,
I walk and slide
over the acorns
and go around
the corner of the school.
Down the hill,
I see a funnel ball game
that wobbles
at the top.
I used to play

with my own rules
counting more points
when the ball
fell through
my favorite color.
The edges are rusty
and the primary colors
are faded
but it still has purpose.

I look at the baseball
fields and hills,
familiar and fantastic.

Trudging along,
there are giant tires
caked with red mud.
They seem misplaced—
stacked up there
in the middle
surrounded by scrap wood.

Coming back, I stroll
past the same indignant trees
I stop to look at their leaves—
scattered, purple onion peels.

This time,
I wave at the trees
and give them
no chance to ignore me.

On Retreat

Azima Lila Forest

silence

cliffs and creek
sun, wind, clouds, snow
moon and stars

i walk the land
i sing and dance
i sit

silence—
only donkeys braying the alfalfa prayer
in the morning
when I step outside the door

weight lifted
past let go
pain washed away
love transformed

new inspiration
in the open air

The Golden Mean

Iris Orpi

Nature's dreams hold you
in arms of mist and sky
you cut across roads of rain
but you yourself
are made of sunshine
and the earth
calls you its own.
It's a brave new world.
Songs and tears
rise from you
fall from you
towards the horizon
on whose colors are
written the consequences
of your deepest passions:
the magnetic magic
of the moon and
the softly whispered
majesty of the cove
coveted by your peace.
You will reach it tomorrow,
right over this mountain
whose gentle shadows
tonight blanket you
in sleep, and whose
subterranean veins
throb to the rhythm
of your heartbeat.
The trees,
benevolent sentinels,
are watching over you,
and through their slender
fingers, the stars
infuse you with
divine energy while
the bonfire dances
in transcendence of

your consciousness.
Your body will commune
with the clear waters
at daybreak;
your spirit will be healed.
The climb, afterward,
will occupy you,
from the skin damp
with life's blessings,
to the awakening flesh,
to the burning core
of your inner immortal,
until you understand that
that climb is your life,
your purpose,
and it doesn't end
at the peak.

And later you will go home,
bones worn,
clothes soiled,
soul pure,
and a different home
will be waiting:
one that you can carry
with you wherever you go,
and never have to
leave behind again.

What is the meaning of drought
Stephen Linsteadt

I wonder, as if the weather is a kaleidoscope
view of our inner life, where vapor trails

pose as clouds in that mocking way
propaganda crisscrosses through bigotry and riots.

What does it mean when reservoirs are empty
and only hope resides on barren shores?

Perhaps drought is the absence of compassion
the view through hungry eyes, our thirst

the bareness of our excuses distilled
into the essentials of what we tolerate:

what our heart knows to be true versus
what our mind refuses to see.

When empathy goes into action kindness condenses
across the jet stream and turns to rain.

***

"What is the meaning of drought" was previously published in *Carrying the Branch: Poets in Search of Peace* by Ami Kaye. Published by Glass Lyre Press, 2017.

The Autarch Snow . . .

Pratik Pandya (Pappee)

Beneath that sheet of white
Are several rusted leaves
Sacrificed, embedded to bow
Towards the autarch snow

Above that sheet of white
Is dense empire of doubts
Lifeless, captivated show
Of the autarch snow

Faces with frozen tears
Ruined laughter and cheer
Manifesting pain and sorrow
For the autarch snow

Nature lost her fight
Between the sky and frozen white
Flawless but full of flaw
Rule of the autarch snow.

Lake Superior
Rachel Gabriel

Take me to the inner sea
where sunlight transforms yellow
into music, and autumn's birch leaves
tremble a thousand golden tambourines.

Take me to our great lake,
a lined horizon blue-grey-blue-
scored water, where the dazzle
band plays sun–wind duets.

Take me here
when I die, where I loved to be
alive, heart full of illuminated
music, mystery's accompaniment,

Take me where
my wind prayer was
instrumental air, each breath
one of wonder.

Our Date with God

Rodger Broomé

Climbing higher into the sky,
Nearer comes the summit.
Drawing ever closer to the cosmos,
Autumn colors Fall all around.
Air crisp and clear,
Our blessed atmosphere created.

Elevated high,
Awesome vertigo strikes deep.
Rock face so chiseled,
The cliff path suspended above the valleys deep.
Autumn colors Fall all around.
Feeling free and unencumbered,
Yet angst about drop.

Awakened dreaming,
Paradise on Earth.
We cannot stay here,
Autumn colors Fall all around us.
Every summer ends;
Toward another Winter; changes come.

The mountain residents are here and there.
Deer grazing, birds soaring, and signs about a bear.
This is not my habitat, but I feel welcome here.
Autumn colors Fall all around.
He invites us "Soon! Come again!"
For Winter's snowfall will close our path.

Memories are made,
And memories fade.
Returning and returning makes things anew.
Autumn colors Fall all around.
Reminding us that all things end.
By faith and patience we will find,
Springtime is just around the bend.

Play with Me

Roseanna Gaye Ross

Come--
Play with me--
We'll chase through fields of daisies,
Play hide-and-seek in the forest grove,
Stretch out in the deep, cool grass,
Tell stories written in the clouds.

Come--
Play with me--
We'll skip over rain puddles,
Sing nonsense songs,
Draw pictures of castles,
Capture lightning bugs in a pickle jar,
Talk and laugh into the dark night.

Come--
Play with me--

But, the child has grown into the man, the woman...
Our fields and forests are lost from life's map.
Our songs and pictures are heavy with reality.
Clouds share no stories,
Nights invoke us only to sleep.

And yet, a voice,
calling out softly
coaxes...

Come--
Play with me--

Cemetery Walk

Sandra Lindow

Early April rain beads waterproof jackets; as we walk past Butch's Bay, a strange cloud rises three feet above slushy backwater ice then dissipates to mizzle. Though icy water shivers the shoreline, a crew of die-hard ice fishers hunch on stools, looking from a distance like half-drunk, backwards question marks staring into holes. "Who would want to do that?" we say, with that certain smugness of long-shared opinion.

We cross the land bridge and up stone steps into Evergreen Cemetery where the dazzled dust of centuries rests among temporarily soddened stones. Our boot soles squitch along muddy ribbons of a broken pale green gown winding between rows of old and new markers, suffering and attachment made tangible above these final homes.

On our right is the grave of a good woman who was once my mother-in-law; up ahead, a sleeping lamb marks the grave of a three-year-old who died a hundred years ago. Around the curve, an ornate concrete tree trunk celebrates the abbreviated life of "Our Beloved Lena."

What is it we carve in each other, as decades slide silently past, the slip of almost unfelt knives shaping our stony epitaphs? Memory's amorphous mist answers, rises from the lake where it was cast, separate stories coming together, moving away each step we take. Black birds line tree limbs, stalwart, rain-coated spectators of our meager parade. "Why do you do that?" I ask a fisherman heading

back to his car. "Hey," he says, "It's a beautiful
day."

Writing

Scott F. Parker

Sand like ash
on this soft
October river.

I'm half-
way to the third-
point of this
current piece
of forever
and there are only
these leaves
yellow and crinkly
to count the time by.

I rinse blood
from my toe
in the water
and remember faintly
what stillness sounds like.

Someone from above
calls down:
—Hey you,
—What are you doing?
—Hey, hey you there.

Her Rainbow
Gayle Byock

It is afternoon. Dark early, I think.
Splatters on pavers, and geraniums
gratefully receive raindrops
on their red petals. Kumquats glisten
in orange skins, and guavas in green,
washed clean for the squirrels.

Then it happens: that strange yellow light,
Rainbow light. And there she is
 in glorious stripes, her back arched
across the street, above the Santa Monica
Mountains, over electrical wires,
cars, houses—meeting my eyes, finally,
she blesses this house with her presence.

She spreads herself magnificently;
bursting, now fading, fainter
and fainter so quickly. Souls rise
to her arch, Souls rise all over the Earth,
like heat misting from hot sidewalks, cooled
by rain. With them is our Mimi,
a sleek, black cat who must have lain still
in her favorite spot under the lemon tree,
waiting for the rainbow to take her up.

Away her soul flies like a gliding bird.
Rainbow strokes her gently with a brush
blending her colorful stripes into black fur.
Welcomed by the clouds fluffing themselves
to envelope Mimi, to welcome her in.
Rainbow's colors warm her soul, bathed
In rain and light on her flight to the heavens.

A rainy afternoon evaporates, as the sun peeks
out. She is gone with Rainbow. I hope to see her
again soon, every time I see Rainbow.
Goodbye, Mimi.

Minnows

Heidi Elizabeth Blankenship

The minnows
swimming
frantically
in isolated pools
where the Muddy River vanished,
reminded me of you,
Grandmother.

When it came to the end,
there was no talisman,
no prayer, no technology
strong enough.
We waited helplessly
at the edge of your bed
and watched you struggle.

There is nothing so painful
as watching someone die—
and nothing as beautiful.
After all, we are
what we are.

I have come to believe
that even spoons have spirits,
that running through everything
is a universal energy
and that at the base of all life,
whether you are a fish
in an evaporating puddle in the desert,
or a human—
there are only two choices:
living or dying.
Every other decision
is a shade between.

Meditation at Bandon, Oregon

George Such

Eternity doesn't interest me, not
the way this ocean does, its never-ending

waves, each a hand that rolls a galaxy
of dice across the sand, and what comes up,

comes up. I'm not inclined toward Paul's
predestination or Plato's caverned eyes –

I prefer this water's conversation, its birds
and surf, its attraction to the moon. I trust

the way my hands perceive these sea stacks
that tower over me, their warm basalt,

pocketed and smooth, carved by gods
of time and chance, the rasp of air and water,

their beauty jutted up like shrines.
I say this prayer to the water and air.

***

"Meditation at Bandon, Oregon" was originally published in *Pennine Ink,* Issue 35, 2014.

Recuperating from a Bad Day

Helen Ruggieri

After the thunderstorm passes
I go out to weed
pulling up stubborn plantain
or millet growing from seeds
birds drop from the feeder.

Yanking out hapless sorrel,
invasive ground clover,
cutting into the sharp dividing line
between grass and garden.

I smell wet earth,
penetrating odor of phlox,
the doggie odor in the grassless place
under the apple tree.

The stiffness in my neck works loose,
I forget the names of things,
pull up root and all from this
rich, composted soil.

And just when I can't tell the difference
between flower and weed
I let that last knowledge
percolate into the earth

falling like rain
on weed and flower
at this moment,
all exactly what we are.

Along the Rocky Branch Creek
Joshua Davies

Some things are just too beautiful;
they must be contained or
the world would be subsumed
right here, and
transubstantiate.

And wind would not dimple
long beds of prairie grass
encircling the fawn.
And sun dogs would not glisten
across moist eyelids in
the musical breath of a cold afternoon.
And clouds in the porous distance
would not bend low
to grace the moon-licked hillside.

And your eyes, dark pools,
could no longer astonish me:
waterfalls dense with translucence,
a violet fire.

Puerto Vallarta, Mexico

Janée J. Baugher

In a basin of fawn sand, a beached pelican,
wings folded as two vast fans, her beak
vacant: opening and closing.
I pray death finds her by morning.

•   •   •

Black pinhead eyes ornament the stairwell,
I count the floors by geckos.
Unable to measure our intent, they scuttle away.

•   •   •

Seen from my tenth-story balcony
in the pistachio-blue sea, two manta rays –
their fins as sinuous as wings in air.

•   •   •

A crab ambles sideways under foot,
adobe bodice against adobe sand,
subtle grains flying up.

•   •   •

I prod a coconut in the tree: twenty-pound,
green round. Machete-scalped,
I carry it away, drain two pints of clear liquid
and eat the fruit, white as linen.

•   •   •

By morning, past papayas trees
and lilies-of-the-valley, no sign
of the pelican corpse, only the excavated grave,
the empty impression.

***

"Puerto Vallarta, Mexico" was originally published in *The Body's Physics* by
Janée J. Baugher. Published by Tebot Bach, 2013.

Healing Space

Katherine Rosemond

There is time now
For rest
Healing

Here
Finally
In the lull
In the wake of the storm
That Raged so long
Wailing
Thrashing
Bruising the walls
In the cold stony deep

Farewell
It is passing away
Beyond the horizon
Of my pulsing heart

Wet sand mush
Holds the shape
Of my feet
Gentle toe tracings
Between rushes
Of sea foam

New steps

Imprinting
Earth's skin
With mine

Mother Ocean's kiss
Salty
Fresh
The wet embrace
Welcomes me home

Surf
Whispering
No need to run...

Not anymore

Tendrils
Of Hot exhalations
From deep
In the ground
Enfold my limbs
Slow motion fall
Drifting down
Shimmering sands
Receive my body

Sun's caress
Touching
Warm fingertips
Slowly
Gently
Spreading open
Nourishing
Each cell

Medicine
Infusing
Oozing in
I sleep
In the arms
Of the shore

The Offering

Lynn Scozzari

Earth, wind, sky, clouds, rocks
Have me,
If you will.
This body – no longer young
Not quite old.
From the Earth we come,
To the Earth we'll return.
In the meantime,
Let me walk among your tall trees
Sip from streams, untouched
Until your grassy knolls become mine.
Nurture me – nourish me.
I'll absorb your iron from ages-old rocks and
Oxygen from breezes that whip wisps of hair
Valleys will covet and cover
Exposed no more
Take my CO_2 and the epithelia shed from my aging skin.
I'll absorb,
I'll repay
As I walk on your rugged terrain.
I won't cry – but if I do – the salty tears will nourish you, too.
Take me in,
Take me up.
I'm yours,
Always.

To Live by Water

Jayne Marek

is to practice deep breathing
as clouds flex over tousled earth

winds unlace willows and clash the ash leaves
as sparrows burst up

not knowing they will die someday
even under a godly eye

the fire of summer probes a creek where small fish
dart like thoughtless words

frogs rev their voices and listen for the slow
sweep of a heron's foot

when a hawk's shadow flies tying sky
to shore and water   self and other

all four elements visible around this pond
a bead shining on the world's ear

***

"To Live by Water" was originally published in *The Tree Surgeon Dreams of Bowling* by Jayne Marek. Published by Finishing Line Press, 2018.

Observations Bring Hope on an April Day
Jeannie E. Roberts

Near bracts and stalks, along the fade
and wilt of cattails, buffleheads float
past the stems and remnants that hem
this pond, dive midst the subtle shine
of slate-colored waters, blur beside
stands of withered remains where
sequined light capers beyond the traces
that embody a season of leavings. Here
in prismatic greens and purples, drakes'
crests shine—their plumage reflects
in spills of black and white as mates
blend in feathered waves of grayness.

Midst the graying wilt of my heart,
where loss stalks, blurs beside a season
of leavings, I stand near the shining spill
of ducks and I'm reminded of spring—
how the stirrings of Earth crest green
and the journeys of birth crown purple,
how dawning's trace every stem,
embody each remnant in prismatic
waves of abiding light—its legacy rises,
in luscious intervals, in the gracious giving
of existence.

***

"Observations Bring Hope on an April Day" was first published in *Blue Heron Review* (Issue 1, Winter 2014). This poem also appears in *Beyond Bulrush*, a full-length poetry collection by Jeannie E. Roberts. Published by Lit Fest Press, 2015.

Of Sky and Earth #28 *by Stephen Linsteadt*

The Courtyard
Michael A. Griffith

A patch of Eden enclosed
by four brick nursing home buildings.
Grass greener than any she could remember,
the cherry tree's bark darker than her eyes,
the tall irises a yellow matched only by the sun above her.

It is Betty's first trip here.
She has been in the home two years now,
but no aide, no nurse, no family member ever took her here.

She grows brave one Wednesday afternoon
when Bingo feels stale and follows me
out to the courtyard, follows me
out to a sunlight so bright
she is blind a full two minutes.

I see her as she stumbles with unsteady steps,
take Betty's thin arm as she mumbles "how good, how good—
the air, it's so good."

I guide her to a bench and wheel my chair next to her,
her tears the most real thing about this afternoon moment.
Blinking, wiping her eyes, Betty marvels at this place of
small mulched gardens, mowed grass,
a gray path between buildings, and a few trees.

The cardinal's calls, the robin's cheerful song,
a chickadee's cocky whistle are better than Perry Como,
Tony Bennett, or conversation for Betty as we sit there
in spring's warmth.

And paradise is shattered by a nurse:
"There you are! I was in a panic looking for you!
Time for your medicine."
Pleas to take her pills out here fall on deaf ears.
Scolds, contrition, bargains for more time in the fresh air,
in the sun, among the irises.

"It's better for you inside,"
barks the nurse, guiding Betty like a child.

She looks back a me, new tears streaming
as the robin flies off and the cardinal is silent.
Only the brave chickadee chirps in protest at the nurse.
I say nothing knowing I will help Betty find
the courtyard again soon.

Bingo is no healthier than a quick trip to Eden.

Spoons & Tonics
Tricia Knoll

My growing-morning-light dream of spoons,
cherry-wood your cousin carved for you,
lengthened into the paddle oar
of a kayak thrust through black waters
of Mist Cove to the glacier-melt waterfall
over kelp-black rocks.

Tarnished teaspoons reached to the prim-lick lips
of our foremothers in white dresses, a ruby elixir
of snake oil tonics' mix of cocaine, heroin
and cannabis with hints of raspberries,
camphor, cinnamon, and rhubarb.
Soothing spoonful, slick to tongue
to keep the mouth silent, hold cries
bottled into dozy head-nods and bobs
that made the babies sleep.

Coming from sleep that left me tired,
what new ladle, dipper, scoop might pour
me, wake me to glimpse again that blade
that sliced the still water of an Alaskan bay
and soundlessly took me forward
to sing by the waterfall
where healing rained.

I Thought I Could Be More
Jennifer L. Highland

I thought I could be more
than just speck among specks,
a piece of the day's moments,
like that cricket among crickets
whistling its one note
in the garden above.

Yet here I sit
desiring nothing
on cool stones
where brook water pours
its endless smooth sheath
from pool to pool,
water and air defined
by a few circling needles
and darting striders
denting the surface with their feet.

The shallow bottoms are grainy
with slow dark life
and there the caddis fly larva
reaches exploring arms
from its tubular house,
soft body enclosed
in bits of leaves
flaking bark
detritus of the water-bottom.
Nosed by tiny whiskered fish
it rolls and creeps.

The sun soaks down in
measured drops
between the leaves
to where I crouch,
my face turned downwards,
thinking: I too could live

wrapped in the small things
of the day—

hemlock needles
shadowed moss
sparrow chatter
grains of feldspar
ripple of light reflected
on the birch's leaning belly—

my soft body drinking.
Naked and entire.

***

"I Thought I Could Be More" was originally published in *Atlanta Review*
(spring/summer 2006).

Restoration
Jennifer Lagier

Depleted spirits recharge
during an afternoon walk
among white sage,
pliant willows,
along lazy kinks of river.

I explore sand bars, silted snags,
remember fishing here with my father.
During autumn, battered salmon swam upstream,
gills heaving when lifted off hooks,
their journey to old spawning grounds, interrupted.

Dad is gone; mom, terminally ill, will soon join him.
I return to childhood's compromised sanctuary,
assaulted by grief and anger,
wash away emotional pain
soothed by restorative water.

A Fehér Hattyú (The White Swan)

Ken Allan Dronsfield

On the small lake outside of Budapest
a sunny Sunday morning and cloudless sky
the old swan takes her final breath as
fuzzy cattails bow in solemn silence.
As her life slowly slips away, a single small
white cloud appears, a vision of her mate
taken by a fox some years ago circles,
the lonely old white swan slowly dies
No one comes to pay their respects
weeping willows shed unseen tears
and the old swan takes a final breath
Mallards fly by, and the hawks stay high
painted turtles glide as grasses sway
whilst children stand on the bank and cry,
church bells sound in the distant valley,
the swan gently closes her eyes and dies.

The Warm Stone Temple
Larry Graber

The warm stone temple
Holds space for me

Yellow sun
Desert bloom
Still cradle
Wind

The air is dry
Old streams talk
In whispers

Spirit Rock
stretches
under me

I chose here
This space

Expanse
Clearing

The waters
from earth source

Rising
Slow
Pooling

For my spirit
Bath

Mother brings
Me the gift
of bird speech

Silent
Talking
Awake

Forms and Products
Ndaba Sibanda

the singularities of the physical world
the wonders of the plants and animals

the phenomena of the landscapes and all
the spectacles of the forms of the earth

is it not the animals` second nature to love?
is it an accident of nature that they die too?

old age or diseases or spells or natural causes?
we try to understand the nature of a problem

Wisteria from Seed

Jeremy Cantor

"Almost no one grows wisteria from seed,"
 I told my sons.
"This one has a healthy set of leaves
so it ought to flower
in about ten years."

 I'm sixty now.

When I was in school
a botany professor showed our class
a bamboo plant.
"This flowers every forty years," he said.
"I won't be here to finish the experiments
I might start now.
If any of you are planning graduate studies,
please see me after class.
I've got some ideas I'd like to try."

I never thought myself a man of faith
yet I grow wisteria from seed
while others study bamboo
plant vineyards
grow olives
raise children.

***

"Wisteria from Seed" was originally published in *Wisteria from Seed* by Jeremy Cantor. Published by Kelsay Books, 2015.

Prayer
~for my sister
Jessica Lynn Hovey

        Tonight
I go barefoot,
run through new grass
its hundred thousand fine blades
soft and chill with dew, welcome
hard gravel pressing up, searing
the day's heat into my soles,
splash through spring's first puddles
until I can no longer feel. Until I feel
everything. Now I understand
how neurons send their signals,
rushing electrical impulses
speeding down axons, relaying
the message to run
how you
        cannot.

Too many neurons
dead, absorbed before
they could tell your legs
to carry you over rubble
and stone and sweet
cool grass.
I wish

        your feet calloused

Sunset II

Murray Alfredson

The sun is set; the cloudscape once softly drawn
  in gold and rust now fades to a single grey.
    All glow has gone; the wind bites coldly.
      Bear with your sorrow: the dawn comes slowly.

***

"Sunset II" was originally published in *Friendly Street New Poets 12* by Steven Brock, Margaret Fensom, and Murray Alfredson. Published by Wakefield Press, 2007.

Winding
Joan Wiese Johannes

Venus still shone in the pale blue sky,
but I dropped my eyes to watch the flight
of a silent crow, and when I looked back,
she was gone; it doesn't matter.

I am not guided by stars.
I follow the zigzag of rabbit tracks, steady gait
of coyote, and little crosses made by birds
whose names I do not know.

They lead me toward the boardwalk
that weaves over ice-covered snow.
I intend to reach the vista
in time to see the sun climb into this world.

A hawk glows on a skeletal tree.
I am inconsequential to him; at least
he seems to take no notice as he flexes and flies
toward the place where the sun will rise.

This is my time for prayer and contemplation,
the time when I am certain that there are trails
we choose and trails we do not choose,
but really, there is just one winding trail.

***

"Winding" was originally published in *Free Verse*, August 2006.

"Winding" was also published in *Sensible Shoes* by Joan Wiese Johannes.
Published by New Dawn Unlimited, 2010.

The Woods

Paul Thiel

Mother died. I went to the park.
Stayed 'til evening when magic's most accessible.
Owls punctuate the darkened atmosphere with somber tones.
The branches above wrap around my spirit
rising into their lair. A nest.
The trees are my siblings since first
I was free to wander there.
So I lean against my brother and whisper,
"Thank you." The limbs above radiating out
support the luminescent roof. My cathedral.
Here I am comforted.   In other cathedrals
the columns fake the trunks of mighty trees,
recreating the woods in homage to god.
We are not so removed from forest primates
and ancestors who danced in the woods.
My father rarely attended mass,
"The garden is my church."

Diagnosed with cancer I asked for help
with the medical decision to rid myself
of the unbidden in my soft tissue.
Scared. But there's no wishing it away.
Retreated to the serenity of my real church.
Embraced the gentle family for release
of anxiety. An answer? *Operate* came to me.
I trusted the doctor and nature. While waiting
I went to the city's Forest Park.
The cascading fountains masking all noise.
Breathing, taking in the trees and sky,
phasing out the rest. Harmony infused.

I still wander into the woods. Stand motionless
inhaling the offering. Then, gradually move
into a slow dance, embracing the essence.
I thank it for my recovery.

Then, I recall years ago when nature surely made

itself most accessible. Living in San Francisco,
confounded by its distractions, I'd hitch-hike
on to Mt. Tamalpais across the Golden Gate
I'd get a lift in Mill Valley's junction responding
to a fierce and gentle presence calling me.
Once there I felt *alive* as nowhere else.

Paths on treeless slopes in pastures
where cows followed contours on the steep land
descending to the ocean so far below.
Fences criss-cross here and there.
I saw my first stile, ladder across the fence—
There was a crooked man who walked a crooked mile,
he found a crooked sixpence upon a crooked stile.
The ancient ladder like in the nursery rhyme.
Alone, I expected to encounter Bo Peep any moment.
Then, onward to trees threaded with paths
worn by generations exploring the mountain.
To Native Americans, Tamalpais is holy.
I felt presence on the trails. The gnarled
twisted pines spoke of otherworldly beings,
spirits forming contortions in the tree limbs.
They seemed aware of my perceptions,
offering melodious scents when I trod
on the fallen brown bay leaves by the streams.
Each step became a part of something special.
Some preordained task, long forgotten,
to then be carved into my psyche. I sang,
made noises in a strange language.
Prehistoric memory?   Then I rested.

A remarkable tree bent down to form a seat,
a friend offering a lap. I'd meditate there.
Concern about how long to remain before
the magic dissipated, was dispelled by a call,
some bird had heard me. I was in the right place
at the right time. Could it be a fairy kingdom?
Would the little people appear, ask me what
was I doing there? Or know, and welcome me.
Why not stay the night? I thought. Why leave?
Would real monsters intrude, carnivorous animals?

Or beings transporting me to their dimension?
Would that be so bad? Ultimately, it was the cold
of night approaching, discomfort, that would
drive me back to the city where the momentary
euphoria subsided into a wildness of urban
degeneracy, the mountain a lovely dream.

However, once on Bolinas Ridge of Tamalpais
I felt the magic beckoning again to me.
A slight depression became my stage. I shed
my clothes, placing them gently on the ground,
and gradually moved my arms facing where
the sun had recently dropped into the ocean.
Let the gods invade my soul. Civilization shed
with its raiment, let my arms and legs think
for themselves. It was a wonderful trance.

Suddenly, I felt a presence. They'd have to
accept my dance. As I swung an arm up
I faced whoever was there. In front of me
were a dozen deer, watching me intently.
Motionless. Watching me dance. Noiselessly.

Rainbows

Joe Amaral

I break them
in segments,
stack them in chests.

Chromatic collectives
overlaying
clouded distress.

Beacons of gold
thru shuttered halls
of skin and soul.

For my many selves,
I turntable a shard
and hold it up

to the sun's
beating heart.

Elemental threads
of storm and shine
splice whole again.

Teach me
how to live
permanently

bent.

Up the Draw in Late Spring

Peter W. Fong

up the draw in late spring

two noisy flocks of waxwings
forkhorns, spikes, does with fawns
the hind legs of elk trotting through pines

bear tracks as long as my boot
white scraps of old snow
the ragged blue of sage

with each slow step
my swollen knee complains
until I reach

the aspen grove.

Renewal

John Lambremont, Sr.

Breakers crash on island shores;
fine grains run between ten toes.

Little kids in surf stay little,
season after season, year after year.

Wade out into waist-deep waters;
wait for the seventh wave to come.

Pipers scurry to and fro;
sea gulls swoop and squawk above.

Long walks along warm Gulf sands;
crab hunts by flashlight near midnight.

See the sun come up at morn;
watch the crescent moon go down.

Another anniversary
for two near to seniority.

A Walk to the Other Side

Stephen Linsteadt

A patch of flowers thrust their colors
to the edge of the garden

like watchdogs, anxious in anticipation.

Like a parade route, crowds of flowers lined up
on both sides of the path. I waved

as though I could hear them cheer.
Clouds lined up behind them like tethered blimps.

Birds began to sing, dogs to howl, and children darted
to the scene thinking the ruckus was the ice-cream truck.

I rushed inside to tell my wife.

She was misting her orchid,
listening to it gossip about the parade.

***

"A Walk to the Other Side" was originally published in *The Poeming Pigeon*: *Poems from the Garden.* Published by The Poetry Box, Spring 2017.

Through Radiant Dark

Joshua Davies

We walk the winter night
of blended shadows. Moonless,
we scarcely see each other.

Only the radiant dark,
the swirling multitude of stars.

You take my hand, whisper my name
and I am present:
        one pulse—
is it mine or is it yours?

No wind. In the closeness,
the moisture we exhale
        commingles.

Nebulae begin to form.
The air is still; cold
has frozen out the clouds.

Working for Change in Rural America
Juanita Ratner

Wind
Wind in her hair
Wind blowing through
        her hair
Wind blowing through
        the trees
Wind
Shaking at the trees
Winds of change

Everything feels it
Vast power of nature
Everything shakes—somewhere
Everything trembles
In awe
Is a storm coming?

"You won't fight with her...
    .....will you????"

All the animals huddle together
Fearing the havoc of an approaching
        Storm.
Backs to the wind, facing the
        fences
The reassurance of limits
Boundaries suggesting
            protection

But she
Feels strangely excited by the wind
She too senses the electricity
Of the approaching storm
And she
Has known the One

Who calmed the storm.

In trust
She holds her face
                to the wind
Feeling its toning charge
  upon her soul.

Senses awake and alive
She breathes the fresh air
Watches the seeds blowing about
Lets go of separateness

She too is nature
She too is a part
Just a bigger seed
Blown by the wind

The rain begins
Fresh, soothing to parched nature

And she pauses
Uncertain
For a second

For she
As human
Has the choice

To follow nature
Or to listen
To a nature
Deep within
Hinting at
Possibility

Open
Listen
Love

Wind tamed

By breath
Brings it all
Past fear
Past storms

All the energies accepted
In centered stillness
Manifesting harmony.

***

"Working for Change in Rural America" was originally published in
Searching for My Real Self by Juanita Ratner. Published by Juanita Ratner,
2005.

Holding On
Michael Moats

I'm still holding on,
Not ready to leave friends, but
One day very soon.

Photograph "Still Holding On" by Michael Moats

When Death Calls to Life

Emily Lasinsky

I prayed today,
out loud.
Addressed the Caretaker of Souls,
a title I've never used
but believe in the Essence it belongs to.

There's a lump in my throat.
I swallow, but it remains
I cry, but it remains
I'll eventually talk about this.

The trees are tall, rooted in the same ground I trust.
They see beyond this moment, yet they still weep,
they understand the necessary ebb and flow that births
a new season.

I've been trying to feel life,
alive,
as of late.
I felt life today,
reflecting on a death that was
expected, yet came too early.

I felt life today,
and she told me Her name.

Song from the Woods
Pamela Ahlen

In the boondocks called the Chateauguay
 I ski the woods alone

Skirt the stony brook beyond the beaver-pond
past hemlock ash and pine

Herringbone the hill   glissando down the other side
whoosh   then glide   past sapling beech

Their russet leaves   like percussive wings
prattling on the limb   still holding tight

Until a rowdy wind might cause the petioles to snap
the leaves to drop   but not today

Just gentle wafts to cue their rhythmic chattering
staccato   along the bone of my ear.

Beech riff   maracas to my two-ski beat.
How absurd to think I've spent my life alone.

Father, when you call
Patricia Frolander

Father when you call,

let me be feeding horses in the big pasture,
at five below zero,
inhaling scent of alfalfa, breath frosting eyelashes,
years written on my face
not in my heart

or let me be fencing in the west pasture,
pulling up wire from pungent earth
where snow bent its back,
tightening each strand against errant calf,
while meadowlarks greet springtime's blush

or let me be gathering in the hills,
content to drink from a battered canteen
the sweetest water in Crook County,
the Heeler quick to roust the cow from brush,
my mare eager to turn a stray

or let me be sleeping in the old ranch house
next to my partner,
whose gentle snores match my own,
arthritic hands joined
horse-miles and hay-miles behind us.

***

"Father, when you call" was originally published in *Married Into It* by
Patricia Frolander. Published by High Plains Press, 2011.

Autumn in the City
Joan Moritz

The trees on Second Avenue attack the sidewalk
with abandon, shooting sharp-nosed missiles

at the pavement without pity. The warheads
find no soft-earth landing, but Nature anticipates

hostile conditions with her prodigious abundance.
Hundreds of smooth-sided bombs litter the walkway,

fill the tree pits, and lodge in sidewalk cracks.
Most are crushed by the feet of people rushing

to work, oblivious to the assault, inured to seeing
life's potential smashed. The acorns, innards mashed,

unable to germinate, still nourish robins and starlings,
still provide a scent of autumn to all who accept it.

CT ABDOMEN: With & Without IV Contrast

Judith Pacht

We worried boys would see through our flimsy voile dresses (how we loved their cling!) worried our nipples – or something more – might show. We wanted boys to see through the flimsy voile but not all the way to the barely healed scars, the wounded feelings, the way we were oh so much less than, though we acted oh so much more than – talked of Albee & Beckett, not a lot but as though. Later the boys came breath-close & they tasted our hearts. It was not easy.

Given the choice today, Wednesday, I'll take my CT scan neat without contrast, & this time please, skip the evidence of flaw now posted public knowledge on X-ray & Findings: the at least seven liver cysts, the 1.3 cm cyst measuring 6 Hounsfield units in the portal venous phase. No pain. Outside, smooth flesh. One Finding not posted: fear.

Another December Wednesday & the canopy of deep green, a windless blizzard of sharp points flecking, falling, the scatter of splinters, my giant camphor tree dispatched. Only a medicinal scent & pink-fleshed chips. Oak Root Fungus silently ate the roots that fed and held it for fifty years. Orange-vested men grind its limbs to bits, suck them up the chute, haul them off. It's winterwarm, good for growing fungus underground. There's algae in the pond's yellow shallows & the frogs have disappeared.

Free to Be You
Karen Wolf

Layers of who she is not
are sheared off by the west wind
and lie in piles around her.
She stares motionless,
gazing at muddy river water
flowing across colorful boulders.
Cold wind chills her skin, but she knows
the sloughing must continue.
It intensifies this peeling off.
This erosion:
> Parental expectations surpassed
>> yet unrecognized.
> Youthful conformity shadowing
>> her essence.
> Societal shrouds of
>> cut-from-the-same-cloth existence.

The wind subsides,
sunshine glistens upon
her newly birthed reality,
awakening her soul to
who she was meant to be.

The Forest Floor
Linda Conroy

Sometimes I want to sprawl beneath the ferns
that spread like fans above the lush ground shield,
and touch the toughness of the holly's leaf,
admire the hand span of the maple vine.
See foliage translucent in sun's light
caught, geometrical, through stands of beech
and boughs of oak, the forest's middle coat
that lies below the strength and lofty height
of silent evergreens. I'll flop down now
and rub my face in moss, to feel the bubble
of the smallest bud, the least of tiny beetles'
rush to reach the warmth of morning's shine
so I'll remember that the soil of life
is here, that its worth is countless, as is mine.

The Witness Trees
Julia Falk

Along the woodland edges at Gettysburg
the Witness Trees stand,
thick, gnarled, and wounded.
I wonder where in their inmost layers they hold the memory
of anguished screams and mad artillery,
the rush of bullets past their limbs.

They must have been lean and willowy then
with branches stretched wide to the sun.
Today their ragged bark is grown thick over
the grit of battle,
the scorch of lightning,
and the tunneling of wild creatures.

I want so much to be like that,
to bend with the wind
and grow new flesh over my wounding.
I want to stand tall with my patchwork skin and broken limbs,
and send out fresh and sinewy new growth.
Still whole and noble,
a vessel for blended suffering and joy.

How Tender Life Tastes

M.S. Rooney

how tender life tastes

when we know the brief flare
of our own heart's beat

as the breakers by our window
rock us pure and blank as sand

and we enter, find no border
where sleep and waking meet

***

"How Tender Life Tastes" was originally published in *in plein air,* 2017.

Driftwood
Morrow Dowdle

The season's over,
but no one seems to know it:
Not the sun-warmed sand,
the green ocean agitated
by the recent hurricane
and the people swimming in it
while others swarm the beach.
You can tell the ones for whom
summer never really ends.

Here is a zone of neutrality,
passing without trespassing
through the backyards
of fancy resorts and rundown motels,
seaside mansions and RV parks.
So also is the spectrum of humanity
on display: Every form of anatomy,
color, and style, varied couplings,
multigenerational gatherings.

How strange to feel like a forgotten
stick of driftwood on this tide,
strangely dressed and slightly in pain,
not only from the broken shells
beneath my feet.
Where others look, in vain,
for calcified treasure,
all I see is ruin,
the remnants of a former home.

I enter the chaotic ocean,
current snaking around my legs.
I can't see to the bottom of the water,
but trust in its tentative welcome
enough to lie back, cradled
by the waves, no better or worse
than the storm's detritus floating there,

the pebbles massaged back and forth
at the irregular shoreline.

Sunset Walk
Toti O'Brien

See the pretty house
door ajar
light peers through the curtain
shiver
glancing at happiness
you don't own

See the red bougainvillea
embracing a cypress tree
think of happiness
wish it were yours

On the wire a dove
cranes her neck
sense happiness
in your muscles and bones
give it back

yellow blooms on the fence
songs out of boomboxes
father hugs little boy
girl smiles at cell phone
through your walk
pierced, trespassed
by shards of shrieking happiness
you wanted and didn't get

(The sun sets
it all becomes happiness)

When Mud Was Our Friend

Ryan Van Lenning

Remember when we used to run toward the rain

back when we were in love with the world
and it returned the favor?

when we couldn't
let raindrops fall to the ground
without our tongues
getting in on the action

or pass a body of water
or a pile of leaves
without jumping in
and mud was our friend?

Shin bruises
and arms drawn with scratches
numb fingers from
staying out too long

were love bites from the world

and just the clouds in the sky
were a song singing itself?

now, is it that our only sunset
is the one that's a perfect 2×4
through The Device
with Valencia filter
that we heart?

our only storm the one
we can prepare for
adequately
three days ahead of time?

the only mud found
on our Goodyear tires?
Is "no mud shalt touch thy feet!"
our unholy commandment?

I've heard that once in a while
a moon comes out to play

but to see her
you have to put some things away

I don't know if it's true,
but I might
take a peek this month

I just might even try
to run towards some things
and make friends with mud
once again

The River

Sarah Dubreuil Karpa

Grey.

All around me awash in grey
Not just bland, but dirty, grimy grey
Coating me in its silt
Dimming my light, my colour, my glow

It is time
It has been too long
I go to my space, my place to feel anew
My heart knows the way

I sense it long before I get there
There is an unmistakable smell
A calmness in the air
And then I hear it

The roar of the river washes over me
Taking with it all those layers of grey
A thirst I did not know I had grips me
I drink deeply of my surroundings

The water fills spaces that I didn't even know were there
Making me feel whole again
My heart rate slows
My breathing becomes purposeful

Breathe in
Purity, Energy, Potential
Breathe out
Negativity, Uncertainty, Pain

It leaves me replenished, restored
Nourishes my body
Nourishes my soul
I am once again, me

Writing by Firefly
Joshua Davies

You follow the trail then the light
goes out, are not sure precisely where
it will appear again. Only that
it will appear again. And you never lose
that sense of wonder when you glimpse it first,
cannot help but follow it.

Above you there may be a million lights,
many of them brighter;
but not one that fits into your palm,
brushes your skin and flashes lightly.
And not one you can fasten
with your pen and make eternal:
whose shimmer is not extinguished
as the dark clouds roll over,
even as its tiny light
flickers and dies out.

In the Evening the Two of Us

Rick Kempa

In the evening the two of us
kneel before the waterhole
in the creek bed below camp,

filling our bottles. The vault
of the sky opens and down
comes the rain again, big drops

splatting our sweat-rimed shirts,
our sun-burnt necks. We say
nothing, keep kneeling,

filling and being filled.

***

"In the Evening the Two of Us"" was originally published in *Ten Thousand Voices* by Rick Kempa. Published by Littoral Press, 2014.

Go Ahead
Maryanne Hannan

Imagine a baby, mother and father.
Or any tableau you find pleasing.

Picture them sitting on a bench
in dappled sunlight, or playing

on a blanket. Let them hear birdsong.
Let them breathe loamy earth,

the wafting scent of pine.
Don't discard the sentimental

image. Please. It won't hurt you.
It may even cast its lightness

on you. Befriend beauty
and innocence and simplicity.

We owe it to ourselves;
we owe it to that baby.

***

"Go Ahead" was originally published in *Earth Blessings: Prayers, Poems, and Meditations* by June Cotner. Published by Viva Editions, 2016.

Petals
Linda Imbler

Sepals fall off softly, one at a time, floating to the ground
Underneath like silk, a satin welcome
Exposed
Now sun kissed and laid bare; feel the breath of Spring on your stem

The breath of new Spring, connect with the seed
Exposing the rose button
Within this opening; feel the breath of Spring on your stem
So close, the flowering petals

Exposing the rose button
Inflorescence
So close, the flowering petals
Spring's mounting ascent

Efflorescence
Exposed
Spring's breathless release
Sepals fall off softly, one at a time, floating to the ground

Sublunary
Meg Files

> The last destination isn't the final place
> on the itinerary but what happens when
> we get home and try to make sense of it.
> — Pico Iyer

We had already planned our trip before
our father died, so we can't say we wanted
to follow him into alien territory. Yet here
we are, with some 120 words for wind, with
cloud shadows striped across hills, in the Rift
Valley where the tectonic plates meet—and
are separating. We walk in blue shoe-covers
in the orange-tan earth of thermal steam. One
sister and I were there at the end, and we try
telling the one who was on the other side
of the world about the repetitive call he made
—letters, it seemed, over and over. What do
you want, Dad? What do you need? Oh, what?
Our husbands guessed: I'm ready to go. Here
we go to the sea where the whales rise from
the universal blue. We raise our sisters' arms
in the geothermal seawater of the Blue Lagoon,
and in the photo is the reflection of our alien
bodies. My sister makes the sound of our father

at the end and the absent sister instantly knows:
Margaret. He called her, did he see her? was she
receiving him? And I break into tears. Of course,
of course. I guess you had not to be there to hear
him. I don't know why I believed geology was fixed.
In 1963 new island Surtsey rose from the sea, and
within two years sea rockets grew on the shoreline.
We traverse lava fields to the volcano, glacier-covered
Katla striped black and white, its harmonic tremors
presaging another eruption. We enter the chamber
of a black ice cave that looks in my photo for all
the world like my pregnant nieces' sonograms. After
a death, signs appear, the butterfly, the column of light

through clouds, our way to keep a spirit here. Geology
is now. Truth? The signs were always here. And so
the dead teach us how to be awake here in the sublunary
world — these Northern Lights, these tiny purple
flowers on the lava rock by the waterfall, this small
shaggy horse. We are Haraldsdóttir, returned home.

Selfscape
Molly Murray

The path turns:
grassland opens
the hills, pines
unbolt the sky.

A hawk curves:
a lock unlatching,
wilderness unfolding
my tightly packed self.

Acorns, Bcorns and Ccorns

Ted Bowman

The botanical consultant
Directed attention to the object of his study
A patch of grass covered by acorns
Shadowed by the aging parent oak
He picked some for closer study
They're not all the same, Grandpa
Look, this one is green; that one brown
This one has no cap
Where is the cap?
Here's a double, two together,
How do they do that?

Buckets were found
We began gathering and sorting
Look-alikes assigned their own homes
Grandpa, these are not all acorns
They are not all alike
Grandpa, some are bcorns
Others ccorns
How do we decide which are which?

I had, without much thought,
Signed up for this research project
When my daughter was pregnant
Had there been fine print, I would have read
"When one becomes a grandpa
A paradigm shifts
What you see is not always what others have seen,
Be prepared for questions."
Little did I know that being a grandpa
Means seeing acorns differently
This upper-level course
Was taught by a botanist with no shingle or degree
But with eyes, thoughts and questions
I wish more of my earlier teachers had said
Grandpa, look!

Silence
Tasha Cotter

The deer must have known
I ached for a friend.
There's a kind of famine
That comes in autumn –
The afternoon half-light
That allows you to see
Clearly for miles and yet
You won't see the deer
And you won't have that
Gladness. You won't see
What's there, there

Surf
Katie Darling

A moment,
When the water rises to meet you,
As you paddle furiously, arms burning.

Your legs wobble,
And you push with your might,
Will this be the time that I do it?

You almost hear a "click,"
As you lock in your heartbeat,
One with the tide.

At once, you surrender,
Finding the balance,
Of ease and effort.

This time is different.

The power surges,
pushing you to new heights,
Lifting you up,
beyond your expectations.

Standing tall, proud and balanced,
The definition of myself, has changed.

Mother nature is powerful.

And so am I.

Dream Tree Poem

Shelley Lynn Pizzuto

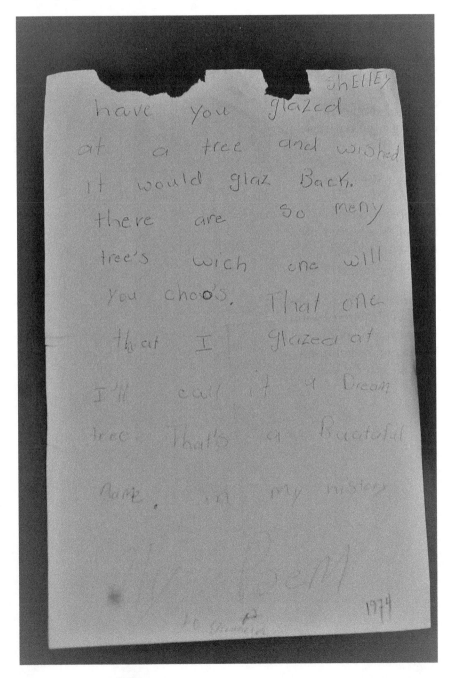

Volcano

Autumn J. Patz

Before you I was stewing
with my demons in the lava,
suffering burns so deep
healing wasn't an option.

You forced them out,
causing a molten explosion.
Smoke, fire,
devastation wreaked
havoc on the moist soil.

My forest suffocated,
my soil was buried alive,
my sky rained ash.
My earth was no more.

But what is often not spoken
after a volcanic eruption
is the renewal of the earth.
Restarting its habitat
after all that choking chaos.

Step Lightly
Gina Subia Belton

Begin again this
Winter morning . . . the Zendo
a refuge . . . welcomes

The doe as she steps
lightly . . . calling one's attention
To humility.

Softened by Shadows, Dusted in Gold
Iris Orpi

May the colors of fall
always be enough

for your pain

for the lost summer

for all the summers
that did not stay.

May these tones of transition
be for you a song
of transcendence,
and may it be enough
to pierce the gloom
of a somber sky
and the hushed light
of a meek sun.

May you find the chance to walk
in the earth's shuffling footsteps
from the lushest of greens
to the vividness of flames
and be ensnared
by the riot of feelings
in between.
May it be the language
of your visions,
the blueprint of your deepest
truths unfurling.

May the short, bittersweet
journey of the leaves
from the branch to the ground
be to your eyes
an exalted dance
of ends and beginnings

of sacrifice and understanding

a treatise on grace,
on embracing the unknown
and unknowable

the movement of time
among beating hearts
suspended
in the brisk air

the telling of a story
whose ending
is unwritten

Hurricane Irene

Lisa Masé

Roses and potatoes on the table,
sprouting blooms and tendrils:

these were gifts left behind
one late summer day
when holy waters swept away
every inch of your land,
from farmhouse to topsoil,
all drowned and strewn
across fields in another county.

That was your last work
with the earth, trowel
and long fingers digging,
tiny thorns, impossible
to avoid.

No one can know
where they met their end.
The petals were prayers
on furious waters
and the tubers bobbed
in the swells.

Night Migrations

M.S. Rooney

When migrating birds
are on the move by night,
some turn telescopes
on the full moon,
study the passing
distant silhouettes
flying before it
and feel the silent
turning of the seasons.

Tonight, here by the sea
in migration season
beneath this Harvest Moon
I watch,
and I think of the dead,
those I cannot leave,
those who will not leave me.

I sense them in currents
beyond the moon,
below the stars,
but can know for sure only
their former destinations,
the dust they were here
that is now part of the sea,
part of me, and I pray for them,
to them, as wings
move silently southward.

Snow
Maureen Ellen O'Leary

Snow surrounds me, sweeping in
from north and south, from east and west.
It falls from newspapers I scan
each morning.
Seeps out of TV screens
each night.
Snow threads through telephone wires and
storms across iPads and cellphones.

A brother snowshoes in the Rockies.
Feet deep in fields of white,
he stops, dazed and dwarfed
by silvered peaks sliding into sky.
Snow blows in from Boston
where a sister captures daybreak light
in the Commons, the white blanket
all rose.
Later the soft dusting of snow
at dusk
by the banks of the icy Charles.
And a Brooklyn daughter blazes home
through blistering winds of white.

They solace me with snow,
my siblings, my daughter.
Blanketed by its beauty, I drown
in drifts of white, snow-bound, snow-blind
in the sun-drenched California day.

A Poem

Scott F. Parker

on the occasion
of a December snow melt:
the night is still long.

Cold Sun

Geri Giebel Chavis

Cold sun brings this season of your loss to an end,
but is a mourning season ever at an end?
Will even a *warm sun* fill our hearts with
what is missing, gone, now invisible?
Will warm sun bring healing,
like a hot bath,
soothing tired, cramped joints and muscles?

My garden can grow now, but
will I see tulips bloom and *not* think of you?
How you told me they were your favorites
just as fir and spruce were your trees of choice?
Will I ever stop lamenting how fate
stole your brain functions,
left you hollow of memories,
an intact body with a soul that was sojourning so far out of range
that we could not find you at all in the end?

No, the mourning refrain recurs with its painful tune,
but my sad song co-mingles with each dawning season.
My melancholy joins with redeeming exaltation--
when evergreens wear their billowy snow-sleeves,
when lilacs keep their purple promise once again,
when cheering bird chirps catch me unaware
on that first green-gold day,
when rustic hillsides flush
with autumn's warmest colors.

Pulling
Sandra Lindow

the last of the carrots
on All Saints Day, was fitting,
for from earth all saints arise,
to earth, all return. Certainly carrots
are saints, upright, purveyors
of necessary nutrition. Lifting them
from dirt, I thought of the Sistine
hands of God, and the tiny turtle
I rescued in Menomin Park, how I
lifted the nearly weightless body
and saw myself hawk, saw myself
the hawk's hors d'oeuvre,
gone in a slippery gulp.

Alligator snapper, I thought,
examining shape of shell and tail—
primitive hater of human hands
whose vicious uncoiled anger
could someday snap my hand away,
but not today and worthy of life
this glorious, sun-knit day as it floated
motionless, alert between my thumb
and middle finger, a small, dark cloud
moving across pine cones
and fallen leaves to be released
on the lake shore, returned to the
hands of the earth as all days
turn toward All Saints Day.

***

"Pulling" was originally published in audio format on *2017 Halloween Poetry Reading* (https://www.sfpoetry.com/hw/17halloween.html), curated by Ashley Dioses. Published by Science Fiction and Fantasy Poetry Association, 2017.

Diagnosis
Sophie Cabot Black

How to be there, still at the center
Of where you first heard – washing dishes,
Late afternoon, the window.

No noise but the clear travel of water
Over your hands. This is how you come
To know heaven, when it is no longer

Possible. The sudden tilt of landscape
Into the one direction, the telephone
Put down. Now, to say it, word by word

Before someone else does, so when you are brought
Back by a child at the table, the dog
At the door, it is to explain this world:

The meadow you meant to walk all year,
That part of the woods you've never been.

***

"Diagnosis" was originally published in *The Exchange* by Sophie Cabot Black. Published by Graywolf Press, 2013.

Etched on the Sun

Victoria Bowers

The stars found their peace high in the sky.
The moon looked across the universe for the sun's guidance.
The sun wandered across the horizon keeping her glory for all to see.
Each day, the stars, moon, and sun carried on a beautiful dance as
symbols of hope.
Far away, he watched gazing at the beauty of the earth.
He watched each sunrise and sunset holding on to the changing light.
She found the sun, moon, and stars.
She grabbed them all and let them rise within her.
Rest now that she holds them.
Her beauty lies in the landscape of that glorious dance made to give
others joy.
Their secret will stay hidden until another one illuminates.
They found their peace high in the sky, their hope in the landscape,
and their joy in the dance.

January Calling

Susan Roche

> *It is finished in beauty.*
> *--Navajo Prayer*

The year, too full,
falls into my arms
before I am ready

so I retreat into
the tended loveliness
of gardens

where I walk
and walk.

I walk while stage-4
cancer sponges
Ouida's bones.

I fold
this stillness
into her beautiful name.

At the waterfall I pause
to soften the echo
of Mia's quarrel

with her niece,
who killed herself
the next day.

Under this silver air
I bow low
to the donor,

alive today,
of Maggie's
new cornea.

Snowdrops rise
through ice but every path
is long.

Kate and I have sung happy
birthday to her son 13 times
since he overdosed.

I invoke him here in
the soft water landings
of geese.

I wonder how bare
birches curve so tall
over the pond.

Abbey's bullied son
refuses school. She wants
her bare life back.

When Karen's love left
with no warning
she had to short-sell

their big house. She aches
for the illumination
of early jonquils.

Rosy blossoms cloaked
these apricot trees
while Minerva's

uncle died alone,
three weeks
before he was found.

Kay's brother,
Lance's mother,
George's sister,

Nick's mother-in-law:
they also die
in January.

We will never
be ready but we are
all something else:

we are knowers
of each other's
names.

Circling the grassy
labyrinth, I dream you
as you whisper me.

Beauty-bound
I walk inside of you
who are inside

of me calling,
calling,
calling our names.

In the Parkway
Susan Weaver

How many times we've run
across this covered bridge,
these city parkway trails,
shared in measured breaths
what filled our minds.
But time lapsed, paths diverged,
I no longer run.

Now you need an ear, talking
more than training, so we walk

among bare branches twined
with bittersweet. You sigh and speak
of job loss, starting over,
how you missed
the warning signs. I listen
as November sun
and a brisk pace warm us.

Then – unexpected – a hawk
dives into leaves beside the trail.

As one, we freeze, scarce dare
to breathe. We note the whitish breast,
the tweedy wings – rich mosaic
of sable, chocolate, tan.
Above the hooked, efficient beak
we note its yellow cere, bright
as the Norway maple up the trail

and keen eyes trained on us.
One swift flap, the airborne hawk shows

empty talons. We hear a scurry,
glimpse the squirrel's tail
escaping like lost opportunity.
The bird drops back. Slowly

it turns, spreading its auburn fan.
"A Red-tail!" you whisper.
"Hunting here, so close!"

Then a wry smile. "Sometimes,"
you add, "even the hawk misses."

Return to Magnetic Rock, Northern Minnesota

Suzanne Rogier Marshall

Only charred skeletons remain along the path
we used to hike. Black trunks scrape the sky,
pinecones clenched on charcoal limbs.
When I was little you held a cone,
told me for the seeds to sprout the tree must burn.
Now, your ashes and ashes of pine mingle somewhere
in this once-woods. Stone cairns mark the trail
across raw outcrops ribboned with shale and Indian flint.
Beyond, exposed ridgelines, snag-stubbled.
And beneath it all, a wash of green.

From a high ledge, I see it—
the glacial erratic rising like an ancient standing stone.
I pick my way down,
past shafts of dead trees into the hollow below.
From ashen soil, blueberry bushes crowd everywhere.
Jack pine seedlings brush my knees.

As I near it, my compass needle spins,
then steadies. North points to Magnetic Rock.
The boulder towers above me—
a lodestone holding old stories: continental rift,
shifting poles, the north of another time.
I press my hand along its fractures, scars
forged by the crush of ice; feel the steady pull,
one body toward another.
Wind stirring through young pine, I hear you
whisper my name.

Peripeteia
Stephen Linsteadt

It happened one day when I leaned on clouds
and they spoke to me of peripeteia—the moment
we realize everything we believe is false.

Clouds are bayonets that way. They don't hold on
to the past or dream of the future—they come and go,
piercing beyond themselves and the sudden reversals of fortune.

I like my clouds full-bodied and improvising.

Clouds take on the form of the land that creates them,
the reason clouds rise differently over a wedding than over
a battlefield.

Blood and tears evaporate together. The effect is seen
in the distance by the awe-filled and the unsuspecting,
when the sun sets and the day's deeds are scribed

in the horde above. No one knows where clouds go
after dark. Perhaps they rock back and forth
in that pleasure dome above the sacred river—

where they wait
to see what our heart creates in the sunrise.

***

"Peripeteia" was originally published in *The Tishman Review: Volume 3* by Jennifer Porter and Maura Snell. Published by The Tishman Review, 2017.

Coexistence
Yvonne Zipter

We are very pleasant here,
the rolling breeze,
the chimes musing in the apple tree,
the beaming sun, Iris the dog, and me.
Not a cross word among us,
though we all occupy this one,
same small afternoon—
along with the garrulous sparrows,
the spellbound shadows,
and the African daisy twitching
in the window box.
No words raised in anger—
no words, in fact, raised at all.
Even the pine tree,
with its rapier foliage,
is content merely to wave
its shaggy limbs in greeting.

The Way Home
Richard Widerkehr

Sometimes when I walk home on the road,
mist sits in the hills, dividing their dark green
from darker green. There's the lake,
then hills and mist and hills and sky—
the white mist like a river floating sideways
up the hills, spread out in billows,
thinning into bits and scraps. It's as if
things had become clearer, more themselves.
The gray sky lets in more light than I expect.
It seems so close, piled up on the hills
like a second lake. And someday I'll go
far away, not on a road, maybe deeper
into green and white, and there won't be
windows, doorsills, paper, socks, or spoons.

***

"The Way Home" was originally published in Bitterroot International
Poetry Magazine, Summer 1987; also published in Northwest Poets and
Artists Calendar, 1994 (Reprinted with permission from Arts & Humanities
Bainbridge); also published in *The Way Home* by Richard Widerkehr.
Published by Plain View Press, 2010.

What the Bee Sees
Ted Bowman

A photographer friend does the unusual
He takes photos of flowers from the perspective of a bee
He dives deep inside
Beyond the colorful bud
The surrounding leaves
To see the inner heart of a flower
What the bee sees

I wished for such a camera
I wished for abilities not possessed
I wished for clairvoyance
I wondered how my grandson saw himself
His inner and outer self
I still wonder

What would I have seen
Had my grandson let me inside
Beyond his hardening shell
Beyond his lovable, attractive surface
To his inner voice of yearnings
Wounds of shattered dreams
His desires about relationships
Whatever

Where was his nectar and pollen
What fed his soul, spirit, body
I'm full of questions, sadness
For my grandson searches no longer
For nectar, pollen or people
I'm stung by his dying
Never seeing what he saw

I want to tell him what I saw
From all my vantage points
I want him to know the beauty
I came upon from his early flowering
Until his dying wilt and death

Like a bee, I wanted to see inside his flower
Even though I deeply loved the outer layers

**

"What the Bee Sees" was originally published in *Coalition News*. Published
by Minnesota Coalition on Death Education and Support, March 2018.

Quagmire
Molly Murray

My boots caught in the mudflats
tangled in rusty wire and ancient
twine, slithering sand yanking me down.

My hands grasped emptiness til they found
a firefly, a spark reminding me to keep trying –
we belong to wings and flames.

Breathing with Boulders

Carol Barrett

Skies undulate with the landscape
here – plains curving like blown glass
while tumbleweed skip the road,
bump along like gyroscopes
catching in the sage. Patches of snow

still cling to earth where rocks
shelter them from the afternoon
sun. Ahead, three horsemen, and dogs
guiding cattle down the gulch.
I slow, then slow again, keeping

pace with the land where I have come
to let the losses of the last year
roll out, their shadows lending
a cautious look back. Already
in the rear-view mirror the clouds

have turned steel blue. Now the cows
wend across my path, despite
running dogs barking commands.
I slow, and slow. One chocolate cow
meanders in front of the car, stops.

I nod. I wait, the revenant gap
between this one and a swaying
comrade growing. I allow the space
she has signaled, grace seeping
into my braked body like a damp

rain on the prairie. I breathe
with the boulders.
                    Finally,
she resumes her journey, deliberate
as the wind on Highway 31.

Another follows. Another. I watch
the whole lumbering parade.
Such are the guides I am given,
timing exquisite as lichen
tracing patterns in the rock.

***

"Breathing with Boulders" was originally published in *The Trumpeter*, Vol.
34, No. 1 (p. 162-163), 2018.

Secret Lovers
Michael Moats

Timelessly waiting,
You offer an open invitation,
Acceptance of your mood is important.
Not about wants or should be's,
But raw honesty of what is.

Many nights I've spent with you
Embracing the wilds of your darkness
And the stillness of your resolve.
Endless depth,
Accentuated by your shimmering beauty.

Yesterday's forgiven
To make room for today.
Every activity has created this moment.
Rising with loving warmth
You sing to my soul an invitation to see things anew.

You demand nothing,
But you offer a reality
To inquire with a childlike enthusiasm
But respectfully with matured caution.
Your rugged nurturance makes sense.

You teach perspective
And seeing beyond the obvious,
Challenging me to see the shadow.

In your presence
I feel small, yet significant.
A responsibility is calling me
To see your tenderness or experience your wrath,
The reactive side you never want to show.

You sway with flexibility
Under the stressful pressures,
While whispering

Fragrant messages
That calm my mind.

You teach me about patience,
The power of connection,
And the importance of calm.
You teach me to see beyond me.

How you hold me, unconfined.
The space offered,
The patience to be
Is a boundless container of generosity.
Never jealous.

Unjudging, you are
Responsive to my presence.
Your intense gaze can be freeing or unnerving,
And if I can tolerate it,
Both.

You teach me to risk,
To be still,
To experience,
To listen,
And to understand.

Secret lovers,
Leaving no trace.
This reciprocity has taught me
How to love.

Distance Encounter
Louis Hoffman

Your eyes fall upon me
I should be scared
but cannot find any fear...

There is something familiar in your eyes,
and I feel safe

You watch as I move among the trees
Standing firm in staring pose
I want to come close
but reason prevents me

Squatting down, shoulders softly angled
I return the intense stare from your eyes
They are brown, not the familiar blue
Yet, something in their presence
Says it is you

"Amaya?"
Softly, I speak
"Is that you?"
Your stare remains firm
And I, unafraid

I want to come close
Yet hold my distance
I feel you calling with your wolf eyes
As Amaya so often did with hers

I lean back into a tree
sinking to the cold ground as
rough bark scratches my back,
still holding your gaze
You lay, head on paws
With loving stare
'I should go,' I think

But cannot leave this comfort
Of you returning to me

I pull my jacket tight
As the crisp night settles around us
The wild night with all its strange sounds surrounds
But I know you will protect me... your pack
And I sleep a needed sleep
Finding a calm I've been aching for

In the crisp morning I awake
Noticing fresh paw prints
and matted grass next to me
Briefly, you are there
In the distance again
Eyes still on me
Then you run off into the trees
In the distance, you turn back
One more long gaze
As your new pack walks up

Walking to my truck
Snow gently blankets the ground
As I ponder my foolish night
Seeking reconnection in the cold woods
"It couldn't have been her"
Then, in the distance
I hear a familiar howl
Tears bind joy with sadness
It no longer matters

***

"A Distance Encounter" was previously published in *Our Last Walk: Using Poetry for Grieving and Remembering Our Pets* by Louis Hoffman, Michael Moats, and Tom Greening (Eds.). Published by University Professors Press.

Quenched
Kai Siedenburg

This time
last year
I saw
withering,
water-starved
plants
everywhere—

their leaves
drooping,
turning brown,
even dying.

I felt
their pain.

Part of me
withered
with them.

But this winter,
it's a different story—

now
we celebrate
the long-awaited
return
of abundant
rainfall.

The plants
drink in
cool, clear
water;

I drink in
the sight
of lush green leaves,

the scent
of moist dark Earth,

the sound
of flowing water.

We are
quenched.

***

"Quenched" was originally published in *Poems of Earth and Spirit: 70 Poems and 40 Practices to Deepen Your Connection with Nature* by Kai Siedenburg. Published by Our Nature Connection, 2017.

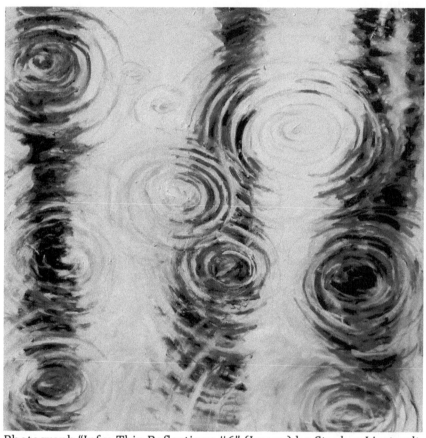

Photograph "Infra Thin Reflections #6" (Image) by *Stephen Linsteadt*

Poetry Activities to Engage Nature

We hope to create some activities that help readers to engage differently with nature than before. These are ideas, not prescriptions. Use them as is or change them to fit your life, your needs. These are not meant as a replacement for therapy, so if you find yourself struggling and in need, reach out to a provider near you. Nature is powerful and has a way of looking into you as much as you look into it. Therefore, choose for yourself how you would like to use these suggested activities in a manner that fits you, your life, your health, your growth, and your healing. The editors of this book are all heavily engaged with nature, but while there are some overlaps, all take different approaches. So, make this experience, this relationship with nature personal. Remember the word relationship rather than participant.

Justin Lincoln is a friend and fellow psychologist who personally has a passion for nature, and he also is a volunteer with a group called *Huts for Vets*. Huts for Vets (http://hutsforvets.org) is focused on providing free 4-day hiking excursions for selected veterans to help them adjust to civilian life through relationship: wilderness, philosophy, other veterans, and with the self. We asked Justin to use the activities while on his trips, and the following excerpts are from his writings:

> I largely didn't write any poems because we did not have a lot of time to spend in solitude. In addition, much of the time I was utterly filled with anxiety as my fear of heights/ vertigo/whatever it is had me on "high" alert. (J. Lincoln, personal communication, April 24, 2019)
>
> Quietly observing my surroundings in the desert, I slowly recognize that the seeming silence is not silent at all, that the apparent barrenness is anything but desolate and empty. So many examples of the tenacity of life, from the translucent scorpion scuttling up the slickrock, to the tree contorting through cracks in the sandstone, rising ever up toward the sun.

Looking at the layers in the rock formations, I'm reminded of the many experiences in my life that have accumulated to make me who I am. Filled with gratitude for the infinite granular influences. Similarly grateful for the powerful forces that have eroded those structures to reveal a singular uniqueness. Just as the persistent winds scour the landscape, polishing features, the breath carves my being into stunning beauty, purifying.

This disorientation, this existential vertigo, reflects a fear of knowing the self and Self. Maybe an underlying, nagging fear of death? Wrestling with an angel until it gives me a new name. Surrender. (J. Lincoln, personal communication, April 24, 2019)

Excerpt from the summary of the trip I related to a co-facilitator, Tim, who could not make this trip:

For me, it was really intense much of the time. Not sure if I had ignored this, or was simply being naive, but of course there was lots of vertical "sauntering." Over the course of the weekend, I climbed up, down, over, and on top of many features of that amazing landscape. Sheer rock faces, tall ladders, across crevices with dizzying drops. My anxiety shot from the top of my head at times. Even just writing about it my hands are getting sweaty again. That combined intensity and anxiety brought the spirituality component of the experience into sharp relief for me. So much vulnerability involved. And trust—in my own perceptions, capacities, and strengths. Trust in others. Wow!

In fact, I felt such strong anxiety for so long during the trip, that I cried at times on the drive home. A release of, oh heck, all kinds of things. Then spent the following day riding through waves of intense emotion. (J. Lincoln, personal communication, April 24, 2019)

I was strongly reminded of these thoughts:

I have spent my life watching, not to see beyond the world, merely to see, great mystery, what is plainly before my eyes. I think the concept of transcendence is based on a misreading of creation. With all due respect to heaven, the scene of the miracle is here, among us. (Robinson, 2014, p. 243)

And the world cannot be discovered by a journey of miles, no matter how long, but only by a spiritual journey, a journey of one inch, very arduous and humbling and joyful, by which we arrive at the ground at our own feet, and learn to be at home. (Berry, 2006, p. 43)

Justin has given the example of making the activities his own, rather than trying to fit into a suggestion. It is much more important to experience nature than to capture it. So, we invite you to take these suggestions and simply use them as a companion as you allow yourself to connect with nature.

Activity 1: Cultivating a sit spot

One of my favorite endeavors is to bear witness to nature's process. To be acknowledged by nature, with a gentle embrace. First, discovery of a sit spot requires patience and exploration. Next, once an individual finds themselves feeling drawn to a secluded, natural setting, they can take part.

The practice is a routine, so the individual must cultivate their relationship with nature by engaging with the sit spot on a daily basis (morning or evening). As time passes, there is a relational shift where nature begins to invite us into its domain. Nature comes alive, allowing us to observe and witness what was once hidden from view.

Activity 2: This Color, This Moment

Whether you're hiking, picnicking, skiing, or sitting at a bus stop, look around you and notice whatever nature is present. Allow a color from nature to present itself and sit with it. What does that color represent in this moment? Try to sit with the moment for a while, and then if your mind wants to reflect on other times let it be. If you take a journey, eventually bring it back to this moment and see what the whole picture allows you to see, learn, feel, and experience.

Activity 3: A Part From/A Part Of

Often we see ourselves as observers (a part from) of nature, rather than interconnected (a part of). Look around and notice how the trees hold the birds, the dirt holds the moisture and nutrients for the trees; notice the food chain that bridges herbivores and carnivores and the oxygen and carbon dioxide cycle. Allow yourself to not just think about these things but to experience the emotions that accompany these thoughts. Notice your breathing and your body's reactions. You are a part of this grand interplay. Where do you fit in nature? How do you fit in nature? What comes up for you as you experience this more as a relationship than transaction? Notice how you remain unique yet—like the rocks, the trees, the water, and the animals—you belong. What is this experience like for you?

Activity 4: Writing in Different Locations

Writing poetry in different locations can help cultivate a sense of presence, or connection to the present moment, and experience one's current environment more deeply. This activity may take place over several weeks or maybe on a vacation, camping trip, or other time in nature. Identify at least 4–5 different locations you would like to connect with that have some significant differences. Take something with you to write in each location. As you begin each segment of this writing activity, spend some time trying to deeply engage your surrounds—the smells, sights, tastes, and all that you can take in. As this connect emerges, write a poem. After each poem you write, reflect upon how the process of writing impacted your connection with this space. As you compile several of these poems, reflect upon them together. See if you can identify similar themes as well as important differences between the poems. You may also reflect back on your time in these spaces as you read each poem and notice if the poem has helped you to sustain the connection with each of these spaces.

Activity 5: Writing as Nature

Identify different parts of nature that you feel a connection with or feel drawn toward. This could be an animal, insect, tree, lake, boulder, or many other parts of nature. Try to assume the perspective of this part of nature and write a poem. You may approach this in different ways, possibly writing different poems from the vantage points of these parts of nature. For example, you may write as a boulder observing the people as they come by and how they treat you and your surroundings. You may also try to write about what is like to be the boulder in another poem. You might write about the boulder's relationship with other parts of nature around it.

Activity 6: Rhythmic Attunement

Locate a tree that is gently swaying in the wind. Place your back against the tree and begin to let your body sway in rhythm with the tree. Let yourself become aware of the smells and the sounds of the wind and the branches. Notice the pressure against you. Do you feel any movement in your feet? Any emotion? Have any thoughts? Continue for as long as you like, and then when ready step away from the tree, turn, and face it. This time allow yourself to sway independently from the tree, yet in rhythm. Again, notice. Write of the relationship, connected and apart, from your perspective or the tree's, or both. Alternatively, you could write of the interplay of all of nature in that moment.

Activity 7: Listening to the Instrument/Orchestra

Mindful presence in nature creates awareness of sounds or the sound of silence. Hike/walk to a place of your choosing and take a position that will allow the most physical comfort. Perform an initial scan of your being (e.g., thoughts, physical sensations, emotions, and stimuli that are "grabbing" your attention). Next, if it is safe to do so, close your eyes and begin to notice all of the sounds around you; take it all in. Select a single sound to focus on. Do not try to force the others out, but simply keep redirecting your attention to the chosen sound. Notice it for 5–10 seconds and then release it as you choose another sound. Notice the second sound for 5–10 seconds and then release it as you choose yet another sound, similar to focusing on a single instrument within a playing orchestra. Continue to release and focus on the various sounds, or *instruments*, until you can no longer distinguish new ones. Once completed, allow yourself to gather all of the instruments and listen to the *orchestra* in its entirety. Continue listening for approximately 30 seconds and then release and choose a single instrument. Notice which one you choose. Notice your body as it reacts to the sound, the thoughts that may come or the blankness, and the emotion that is felt. Release your focus and return to the orchestra. Continue listening for approximately 30 seconds and then release and choose a single instrument. Notice which one you choose and your experience. Release the sound, return to the orchestra, and notice your experience. Continue this exercise for as little or as long as you like. When you are ready, take a deep breath in and out, open your eyes, and perform an initial scan of your being (e.g., thoughts, physical sensations, emotions, and stimuli that are "grabbing" your attention). Write of your experience, your journey, pleasures or frustrations, insights, or your connection to nature.

Activity 8: Nature as a Mirror

The world of nature is perpetually in flux and is filled with transitional experiences. Some of my most impactful lessons for life have come from observing, experiencing, and reflecting on these transitions. As you walk, hunt, hike, ski, swim, or simply sit, take notice of the changes around you. Maybe it is ice melting into the stream, the morning's sun piercing the darkness of night or night blanketing the sun, the colors of leaves changing, life to death or the life that bursts from the remnants of what once was, or from the wetness of a rain shower to the warmth of the sun. What stirs in you? Does this remind you of anything in your life, a celebration or a struggle? Perhaps a sense of trusted safety to being thrown into chaos, or your transition from a lived hell into the life you are creating. How does this experience connect with you? Write a poem that reflects this experience, this learning, or this change.

Activity 9: Life/Relationship History

Begin this exercise by writing a life and/or relationship history of nature. Pay particular attention to how your relationship, feelings, and engagement changed over time. Although you could write this as a poem, it is likely easier to write this as a narrative. After you have finished the history, review it, paying attention to what stands out to you emotionally. When you encounter the particularly emotional moments of the history, write a poem drawing on that part of your connection with nature. For some, it may be helpful to put the history aside for several days or weeks and then review it.

Activity 10: Tree Cycle

In the fall, notice a tall tree that has begun shedding its leaves. From the beginning it has struggled to break free of the darkness of the soil to break through to the light. Yet, this dark soil has also given it sustenance and a place to anchor its roots. Year after year of battling winds, insects, and storms it continues to reach upward and outward, broadening its presence. The more it receives, the more it gives (shelter, food, oxygen). Year after year, buds turn to leaves, leaves expand and are productive, and then leaves fall to the earth to rejoin its birthplace. Notice that many trees offer a gradient timeline, from the greener leaves still more clustered near the bottom, to the less densely populated middle that shares much more transitioning colors, to the top that primarily holds the remaining few dried remains waiting for their time to let go. Hold this reality for the tree, for you, and notice what comes up for you. Notice any discomfort. Notice any meaning. Notice the shared experience. Do you have the same acceptance? If not, what stands in the way?

Activity 11: Cultivating and Preserving Awe
The experience of awe can be a powerfully transforming experience (see Schneider, 2004, 2009, 2019). Nature often creates or inspires the experience of awe. However, in the busyness of daily living, we often lose touch with the sense of awe inspired by nature. Set aside a period of time—such as one week or one month—to cultivate awe inspired from nature at least once a day. This activity can help us embrace the beauty of nature that surrounds us but that we often do not notice or begin taking for granted. You do not need to live in the mountains or by the ocean to notice nature's beauty. Sometimes, we can find the beauty of nature in a tree in the middle of a busy city— *nature will find a way!* When you find this experience of awe, write a poem about that experience while you are experiencing the sense of awe. It does not need to be a long poem; it can even be just a few lines. At the end of the period, spend some time reflecting and writing about how the cultivation of awe impacted your emotions, relationships, and choices through the period where you were daily cultivating awe. This may inspire you to try to cultivate the experience of awe from nature every day—even when you may not have time to write a poem from within the experience.

Activity 12: Nature as a Friend
One of the never-ending feelings I experience in nature is its vast acceptance. Climbing a 14er was when the feeling of openness, accompanied with the requirement of respect, created the feeling of being small but significant. No matter what I am going through or what feelings I have, nature has always been large enough to hold what I bring. However, she never sits passively, and she offers challenges to all that are willing to seek and accept them. How does it feel to be in the woods, near the ocean, sitting in a park, or walking through the desert? What happens if you speak out your struggles? How does it feel to symbolically place your worries on a branch or a rock? Focus on feeling the waves ebb and flow the tension from your body. What challenges does nature offer you? What lessons are shared?

Activity 13: Re-reading *A Walk with Nature*
Try reading through *A Walk with Nature* again by reading one poem a day. After each reading, spend some time reflecting on the poem and how it relates to your own relationship with nature. Mark the poems that stand out to you and, after finishing re-reading the book, return to the poems that stood out as most significant for you. You may choose to continue to re-read these poems over time or during times when struggles, joy, or periods of detachment may occur. Pay attention to how the poems interact with your own living, growth, or healing process.

Activity 14: Cultivating a Balanced Relationship with Nature: Three Practices—Breathing, Mourning and Gratitude
Having cultivated a sit spot, practiced writing in different locations and worked with identifying parts of nature that we may feel a connection to, we may find ourselves prepared to open up to a deeper relationship with nature through poetry. Many wisdom and spiritual traditions—in particular, Indigenous Earth-based faith traditions— remind us that a mindful return to relationship with nature deepens our compassion for all beings, including our living, breathing planet. Opening up to the practices of breathing, mourning, and gratitude with poetry in nature is a portal of entry toward cultivating empathy and compassion for ourselves and all beings. The following practices with nature and poetry are meant to be engaged in order, though you may at times find that as your capacities deepen, one practice may call for your attention over the others. It is recommended to begin with the breathing practice.

    Breathing. Breathing is so simple, right? Breathing with relaxed and focused attention, many wisdom traditions would say, takes a little bit of effort. This practice of breathing with nature is different than cultivating your sit spot and is akin to walking meditation. In some Earth-based Indigenous traditions, walking meditation is practiced in formal and informal spaces, from the tiny confines of a Zendo foyer to vast landscapes of hills and valleys or a busy city street. In the Zen tradition, walking meditation is known as kin hin. This breathing with nature, while just as intentional, is choosing to practice outside with the intent to invite some spontaneity to one's experience with engaging different aspects and locations of nature in relationship to your breath. Noticing our breath in the presence of nature can be experienced as stabilizing and spacious. The essential invitation to this practice is to just notice at any time of day where you are in relation to nature and to take inspiration—literally!

In any moment in your day, stop.

Take yourself outside and breathe an intentional breath. If it is comfortable and safe for you to stand where you are, remain standing; if it is better to sit, then sit. Allow your eyes to drop their gaze to just in front of your toes. Bring your attention to the physical sensation of your inhalation and exhalation while noticing your breath as it moves through your mouth and/or nose and paying attention to the rise and fall of your chest, your belly.

What sensations do you notice? Continue paying attention to your breath, and the sensations that arise, for ten breaths. If thoughts arise, allow them to be, like clouds moving across the sky. After ten breaths, shift your gaze upward, relaxed and open. No need to reach out for any sights in particular, just allow what is present to come into view. Notice where you are. Continue to notice your breath as you take in the landscape around you. Breathing in, what comes into view; breathing out, what is resting in your gaze? Without evaluating, analyzing or interpreting what is holding your gaze, continue to breathe in and out for 10 breaths as you appreciate the landscape embracing you. What do you notice?

For 10 more breaths, allow your awareness to embrace the world that is embracing you. What do you notice? Now take this moment to invite a few words to arise; allow them to bubble up like the gurgles of a stream, gently and quietly. If you feel inspired to, you can jot down these inspirations quickly without giving them too much thought. At the end of your day, after practicing breathing with nature one, two, three or more times, take a quiet moment to explore these inspirations. What arises for you in this inquiry? If you feel moved, explore how you might weave these inspirations into a poem or haiku.

Mourning. Often times, when we cultivate a practice of locating ourselves within nature through the connection of our breath, we may come to notice the many ways we have become disconnected from our relationship in nature. Breathing with attention in nature can connect us to an awareness of our own vulnerability and the vulnerability of others, in particular other species and the planet herself. Grief may arise. Observing nature with the breath can remind us of the impermanence of all living beings on the planet. We may experience the existential encounter that "even I will die someday." This can be a very tender moment when noticing the last leaf falling from a tree or the shades of a green landscape shift to a crackling, dry sienna. While you take this in, it is important to discern between loss, grief. and mourning. One reason for this discernment is to be able to accurately identify what we are feeling. Briefly, loss is the experience of separation from a relationship. Many types of loss occur throughout a human life. Grief, one's reaction to loss and mourning is the essential process for coping with loss and deprivation. All spiritual, wisdom, and cultural traditions have conceptualized, through practice-based evidence, the benefits of ritual and ceremony when coping with loss.

After a time practicing breathing with nature in the way it is previously described, one may integrate a practice of mourning as a way to honor the grief that may emerge. This mourning practice can be integrated either before the inspirational jottings described in the breathing practice above or afterward, when reflecting on these brief poetic notes. This mourning practice is very simple and quite ancient. It is said in some Native American traditions that when we find ourselves without anyone to witness our pain and suffering, we can always ask nature to be our witness. Trees, rocks, and oceans have been a witness to human suffering for millennia. In these tender moments, we may invite a specific request of rock. One Native American tradition says that "when no one else can hear your pain, you can ask rock."

If you are transitioning from your breathing practice to this mourning practice, begin by gently observe your surroundings. Notice where there might be a rock, sitting quietly and patiently awaiting your attention. With respect and humility, introduce yourself to the rock. Invite the rock to be a witness to your current feelings of loss and grief. You might pick up the rock, hold it in your hands, feeling its weight and noticing its shape and colors. Of course, you may find your attention drawn to a rock that is too large, in which case you may sit next to it, rest your head or body alongside. When you feel this rock's attention, you may share the inspired jottings from the previous exercise or quietly speak from the heart what is alive for you now. What is grief speaking to you in this moment with the rock? Sometimes our grief speaks from our sadness in recognizing the ways in which we have not been respectful to nature; share this sorrow. Write a short poem with rock and share it. When you feel that rock has received your sorrows for this moment, bring your mourning to a close. Give Rock your gratitude. Breathe deeply in and out. You may add the poetry from this mourning to your inspirational jottings and gently explore them in the next practice or at the end of the day as previously described.

Gratitude. When we tend to our loss through ritual and ceremony, gratitude is not far behind. From breathing intentionally with nature to coming into awareness with loss and honoring the grief with a mourning practice, spaciousness is cultivated for gratitude. There are many gratitude practices from many traditions, and still I find the humblest practice to be the most profound—the practice of just saying thank you. Indigenous scholar and anthropologist Angeles Arrien was fond of saying, "There are really only three prayers: Help me, Forgive me, and Thank you." These three simple invitations can be taken up after the two previous practices have been tended to or practiced on their own. At the end of the mourning practice we may ask rock, "help me to___" and "Forgive me for___," ending with "Thank you for your bearing witness to my pain." These simple gratitude practices can also be spoken quietly at the end of the breathing practice when transitioning into inspirational writing. On its own, this gratitude practice may be of benefit anytime you find yourself suddenly aware of your location in nature. As you move throughout your day, take a moment to offer a spontaneous gift of generosity and gratitude with a simple thank you to the trees for cleansing the air as best they can, to the water for supporting life, and to the falling snow for uplifting you in childlike joy! As the mystic poet Rumi said, "wherever you stand be the soul of that place" and give gratitude for its very support under your feet. If you feel inclined, you may write a short poem or haiku of gratitude in this moment. It needn't be with pen or paper; this is best written on the heart, from your soul.

Engaging in all three of these practices together invites the ego-centric human experience to cultivate an intentional awareness honoring a balanced relationship with nature. Practiced together or separately, breathing with nature, mourning, and giving gratitude may shift one's perception of a false separation from nature, a view inciting dominion over a wild experience to be conquered, or someplace that we may carry our tent to every now and again. In tending to balancing our relationship with Nature, we are reminded of what Buddhist philosopher Alan Watts says, "We do not 'come into' this world; we come out of it, as leaves from a tree. As the ocean 'waves,' the universe 'peoples.' Every individual is an expression of the whole realm of nature, a unique action of the total universe."

References

Berry, W. (2006). *The unforeseen wilderness: Kentucky's red river gorge.* Emeryville, CA: Shoemaker Hoard.

Robinson, M. (2005). *The death of Adam: Essays on modern thought.* New York, NY: Picador.

Schneider, K. J. (2004) *Rediscovery of awe: Splendor, mystery, and the fluid center of life.* St. Paul, MN: Paragon House.

Schneider, K. J. (2009). *Awakening to awe: Personal stories of profound transformation.* New York, NY: Jason Aronson.

Schneider, K. J. (2019). *The spirituality of awe: Challenges to the robotic revolution* (Rev. ed.). Colorado Springs, CO: University Professors Press.

About the Editors

Michael Moats, PsyD describes himself as a father, a husband, and a friend. His passion as a clinical psychologist lies in working with clients who are learning to redefine their lives and create new meaning, especially those dealing with grief and loss in its many forms (i.e., death, divorce, job loss, recent move, natural disaster, war.)

Michael frequently utilizes nature and stories from his hikes, hunts, walks, skiing, and general sense of awe and intrigue in the therapeutic setting.

Raised in rural Illinois, he saw his father frequently wander through the woods with no agenda beyond experiencing whatever came. His grandmother fished with a cane pole and with the enthusiasm of a child, while his brother taught him to hunt and to better read the woods and the wind. It was Michael's own sense of embracing the silence of nature that offered a symphony of sounds and opportunities.

Struggles in nature, insights from engagement, and the paradoxical realization of how small yet significant each person is in relation to nature has shaped how he embraces life, his perspective of relationships, and his therapeutic work with clients. He would not negate the importance of intellectual knowledge concerning nature, but he would argue that no amount of knowledge can match the experience of being in and having a relationship with nature. He believes that there are not enough days in a life to learn all that nature has to offer.

Dr. Moats recognizes that every experience creates an opportunity to learn, to grow, and to heal. And, nature is large enough to hold whatever one is carrying. However, as one grows to see the immense giving power of nature the resulting relationship also demands that one has a responsibility to return these gifts through stewardship and sharing.

He believes that it is important to see nature through the eyes of a child and care for it as a parent of that child.

Derrick Sebree, Jr., PsyD is a multicultural psychologist and social justice advocate whose work focuses on the intersectionality of race, ethnicity, and our relationship with the ecological world. As a Black male professional, Derrick seeks to illuminate the relationship between ecological and social justice from a multicultural,

ecopsychological perspective. He views the Earth–Human relationship as a parallel, interconnected process to the Human–Human connection, for how we view one another is a microcosm of how we view all modes of life.

Derrick has lived within the city of Detroit, where nature was not viewed as safe; instead, nature was viewed as something to avoid. Detroit has been a city rife with racial and environmental struggle. Over the years, as Derrick has worked to heal and discover elements of himself, he has turned to nature as a guide, beginning with experiences on urban farms in the inner city, to eventually kayaking on the Colorado River, and camping in the Black Canyon. Nature takes on many roles, from guide, to mentor, to nurturer. Nature fulfills all these identities for us, providing a unique experience where one can come to see themselves in nature, and nature within themselves—a reflexive process of transformation and change where one comes to develop a deeper understanding of themselves within nature. These experiences with nature have shaped Derrick's relationship with nature, and himself, to where he now can develop a richer connection to nature as an urban, person of color.

Nature is a mirror into ourselves, casting back the deepest reaches of humanity. Reflecting pain and shadow, transforming to light and beauty.

Gina Subia Belton, PhD is a thanatologist, a compassionate companion and empathic witness in her private practice at Redwood Palliative Psychology, where she focuses on cultivating her community's capacity for living, aging, dying, and grieving well. Oriented in an ecopsychological attitude, Gina's work and research in existential medicine is empowered by her approach characterized as

"cultivating an ethic of radical hospitality" (Belton, 2017). The concept of *cultivating an ethic of radical hospitality* is the ecopsychological out-growth of her Indigenous, Mestizaje lineage and guides Dr. Belton in her work with clients transitioning to the end of life and supporting the beloveds who mourn them. As a professor of psychology at Saybrook University, Gina is an emerging Indigenous scholar and committed to the success of her students growing into their own scholarship and practice.

Growing up in the '60s and '70s in the midst of the confluence that was rural California, Gina played and worked in community with the mountains, rivers, and the rhythms of agricultural life in the San Joaquin Valley. It was this life that nourished Dr. Belton's eco-psychological attitude and passion for social justice, community, liberation, and ecopsychology, in particular at the end of life. Most important, as she played and worked in community, her life was fostered by the core Indigenous values of: 1) Respect, 2) Humility, 3) Vulnerability, 4) Patience, 5) Humor, and 6) Service. These values inculcated Gina's psyche through casual giving and receiving of healing stories and songs, each a medicine and a gift from her large extended family, along with her Elders and Ancestors. This medicine, always a reminder to Dr. Belton that we are not stewards of nature or that we have dominion over nature but that we *come out of* nature, as expressions of *psyche as nature.* As C. G. Jung wrote, "...for nature is not only harmonious, she is also dreadfully contradictory and chaotic" (*Memories, Dreams and Reflections*, pp. 228-29)—to understand this, is to understand that *we* are all relations, jewels in the web of interdependence, within the same sacred hoop of inter-being.

Louis Hoffman, PhD, is a licensed psychologist in the states of Colorado and Iowa, and maintains a private practice in Colorado Springs, Colorado. *A Walk with Nature* is Dr. Hoffman's 17th book. He has also published numerous journal articles and book chapters, most

of which focus on existential and humanistic psychology, multicultural psychology, the use of poetry in therapy, and/or the psychology of religion and spirituality. An established scholar, Dr. Hoffman has been recognized as a fellow of the American Psychological Association and five of its divisions for his contributions to the profession of psychology. He serves on the editorial boards of the *Journal of Humanistic Psychology*, *The Humanistic Psychologist*, and *Janus Head*, and he is an adjunct faculty member at the University of Colorado at Colorado Springs, Saybrook University, and Pacifica Graduate Institute. He also is an affiliate instructor with the Existential Humanistic Institute and provides training and supervision through the International Institute for Existential–Humanistic Psychology. Dr. Hoffman is a husband, father, and dog owner thankful to be living in beautiful Colorado Springs. One of his favorite activities is spending time hiking with his dogs, which he considers a spiritual practice.